Problems of Urban Governance in Bangladesh

Problems of Urban Governance in Bangladesh

Pranab Kumar Panday

SERIALS PUBLICATIONS
NEW DELHI (INDIA)

First Published *2009*

ISBN: 978-81-8387-216-4

Published by

SERIALS PUBLICATIONS
4830/24, Prahlad Street, Ansari Road.
Darya Ganj, New Delhi-110002 (India)
Phone: 23245225 Fax : 91-11-23272135
E-mail: serials@satyam.net.in

Dedicated

To my parents
who have introduced me
to the land of knowledge

And

To my beloved wife

CHITRA

and sweetest daughter

PROTTASHA

who are the sources of all my
inspirations

CONTENTS

Foreword

Problems of Urban Governance in Bangladesh explores an extremely important issue of policy implementation, and sheds light on the critical aspect of coordination in the process. This is a major contribution that will contribute to the understanding of problems faced by urban local governments in Bangladesh, and facilitate the search for their resolution. Highlighting the role of successful policy implementation in the establishment of good governance, Pranab Kumar Panday provides a competent analysis of the policy subsystem of Rajshahi City Corporation to identify strengths and weaknesses. The book should be useful to academics, students, consultants and local government officials.

Ahmed Shafiqul Huque
Associate Professor
Department of Public and Social Administration
City University of Hong Kong

Acknowledgement

I earnestly articulate my gratitude to Dr. Ishtiaq Jamil, my supervisor for his outstanding professional guidance, persistence in questioning and challenging me that finally shaped my ideas. His stimulating suggestions, encouragement and affection always inspired me to my work. I am really grateful to him for his academic support and meticulous job of going through the drafts many times by providing useful comments.

The Norwegian State Education Loan Fund (Statens Lånekasse) funded my study. The University of Rajshahi, Bangladesh granted me study leave and the Department of Administration and Organization Theory provided a congenial working environment. I am obliged to all of them.

Back home, I am particularly indebted to my respondents for providing me their time, patience and attention. I am also thankful to my elder brother, Pradip Kumar Panday for his continuous support in terms of provide me with several secondary documents and reviewing news paper.

My heartiest appreciation to all of my family members for their support and encouragement throughout the study. During the study, I was lucky enough to have the company of my wife Chitra and daughter Prottasha. Their company provided me emotional support, which helped me to pursue such a long course abroad. At last but not the least, I profoundly admit the inspiration, support and sacrifice rendered by my wife for the completion of this thesis. Finally, a special thanks to my little Prottasha who is the source of all my inspiration.

At last I would like to bear responsibility of all errors, mistakes and lack of judgments which I have committed unintentionally.

November 2007 **Pranab Kumar Panday**

1

INTRODUCTORY DISCUSSIONS

INTRODUCTION

What happens to policy implementation when the process suffers from problems of coordination? Who are the dominant actors in the implementation of policy? Does intra-organizational coordination affect implementation of policy? Or is it that lack of inter-organizational coordination hamper policy implementation? This study intends to address these questions by examining the process of implementation of policies of urban governance in Bangladesh[1].

The urban sector in Bangladesh comprises six City Corporations[2] (Dhaka, Chittagong, Khulna, Rajshahi, Syllhet and Barisal) and about 279 secondary towns or municipalities (known as Pouroshavas). Bangladesh has not yet developed appropriate strategies, policies, and institutions necessary to cope with urban governance. The country has typically followed a centralized system of policy making and resource allocations, where the inter-governmental transfers are unstable, not well defined, and lack an adequate system of incentive mechanisms. Inspite of having a legal-institutional framework of a decentralized system of local government, in reality, there has been little decentralized governance at the local level. Besides, lack of fiscal resources and limited decision-making power of local governments, the level of decentralized government that exists have been largely ineffective because of lack of accountability, concentration of power by the municipal executives, obsolete laws and regulatory framework, limited administrative capacity, lack of investment in human resources and weak supervision by the central government agencies. As a result, deficiencies in urban infrastructure and services, including water supply, sanitation, solid waste collection, drainage and transport range are severe and at times extreme.

The specific purpose of this study is to explore how intra and inter organizational coordination affect the policy implementation of the urban governance in Bangladesh and identify the factors that affect co-ordination in the policy implementation. Here, I will try to discuss the problems of co-ordination in the implementation of policies at a City Corporation in Bangladesh.

STATEMENT OF THE PROBLEM

Successful implementation of policies is a prerequisite for the establishment of good urban governance. Policy implementation usually takes place in cooperation with other organizations. Similarly, when it concerns urban governance in Bangladesh, City Corporation requires to cooperate with several government departments such as Power Development Board (PDB), Roads and Highways Department (R&HD) and Local Government Engineering Department (LGED). Therefore, urban governance in Bangladesh is highly dependent on fruitful and useful cooperation with different actors.

Coordination is a complex and crucial issue that is needed both at the day-to-day operation level and at the policy level. Problems of coordination occur due to involvement of multiciplicity of institutions and their overlapping nature of jurisdictions. One research indicates that at least forty-two institutions are involved in Dhaka Metropolitan Area (DMA)[3] with different facets of urban development activities (Mohit, 1992:101, cited in Khan, 1997: 16). Lack of cooperation and coordination between municipal governments, on the one hand, and special government bodies, special development authorities and special purpose authorities, on the other, is that the former are elected bodies while the latter are government agencies whose nature of operation and system of reporting decisions are different. However, this acute problem of lack of coordination has also to a large extent made it difficult for the municipal corporations to implement various policies and to solve the problems of their clientele (Khan 1997:16).

Lack of coordination creates a lot of new problems such as failing to meet deadline of a project. As the deadline exceeds, the cost of the projects increases. Accordingly it becomes problematic for the City Corporation authority to start new projects. All these problems in a way deprive the citizen from availing the opportunities of good urban governance. It is also evident that many of the development projects remain incomplete in the middle stage due to problems of coordination. This is evident by the following examples.

> In 2003, the World Bank withdrew nearly 50 per cent of USD 220 million allocated grants for the development of the transport infrastructure in the Dhaka[4] City that was a clear sign of the donor institution being disillusioned with the progress made in its implementation. The fund cuts had led to dropping of two major components of the plan, the first one having to do with reduction of traffic congestion and the second with pollution control. This happened because of lack of coordination and understanding between Dhaka City Corporation (DCC) and Roads and Highways Department (R&HD), the two principal agencies involved in the projects. Both the organizations were blaming each other for the World Bank decision to withdraw funds. Obviously, they were trying to hide behind their failures by passing the buck against each other (The Daily Star, 12.03.03).

The dependent variable of this research is policy implementation. Here, policy implementation refers to the implementation of the infrastructure policy of Rajshahi City Corporation (RCC). Efforts have been made to identify involved actors in the policy implementation process and to analyze role of coordination in the implementation of infrastructure policy. Coordination has been used as the intervening variable. Within the organizational boundaries of RCC, there are various departments responsible for different activities. On the other hand, RCC deals with various government departments in regards to the implementation of infrastructure policy. So, coordination in terms of intra and inter organizational coordination, is inevitable for the effective implementation of any policy. Coordination is influenced by various independent variables such as lack of institutionalized rules and regulations, financial management, central-local relations and democratic versus bureaucratic accountability.

Institutionalized rules and regulations are important because these specifically allocate responsibilities among involved actors and guide them regarding who would do what and how. Lack of institutionalized rules and regulations often give birth to conflict among involved actors as it does not provide any direction to the actors. RCC is a hierarchic organization as every decision needs to be approved by the Mayor. On the other hand, the existing law through which RCC administer, is ambiguous in many respect. Problems of coordination take place due to overlapping and misuse of these ambiguous laws. Financial management has a far reaching impact on the problems of coordination. RCC suffers from inadequate financial resources as the central government grants always fell short of actual needs. Therefore, it becomes difficult for the authorities to distribute scarce resources among contesting departments. In such a situation, frustration and conflict grows among different departmental heads that in the long run create problems of coordination. Central-local relation is also an important variable that influence coordination in the implementation process. Because, successful implementation largely depends on the extent of autonomy that the central government allows to the urban government bodies. If the central government tries to exercise more financial and administrative control over the urban government bodies and local government bodies vie for more autonomy and resources, problems of coordination happen among these two organizations that might affect the policy implementation. The contrast between democracy and bureaucracy also affect coordination as they differ in accountability pattern. The nature of the accountability of the City Corporation is bottom-up which means that City Corporations are accountable to the people for their activities. On the other hand, accountability of the government agencies is top-down which means that the officials are responsible to their superior bosses. These differences of accountability often foster problems of coordination that affect policy implementation.

SIGNIFICANCE OF THE STUDY

A number of researches have been initiated over the years on the issue of coordination. Most scholars have tried to concentrate on either intra-organizational coordination or inter-organizational coordination perspective. Among them, are Mintzberg (1979) and Van Meter and Van Horn (1975). Mintzberg has emphasized on the intra-organizational coordination mechanism. He tried to analyze what type of coordination mechanism is suitable for which type of organization. On the other hand, Van Meter and Van Horn stressed on the inter-organizational communication network. They argued that inter-organizational communication network is essential for the successful policy implementation. This study is a step further from both the streams and tries to find out causes of intra and inter organizational coordination problems and its impact on the policy implementation.

The study is concerned with policy implementation of urban governance in Bangladesh. Since the basic objectives of this research is to study and explore the problems of coordination in the policy implementation, therefore, the study sheds light to identify those actors who are entrusted with the responsibilities of implementing various policies of City Corporations. The City Corporations deal with various organizations (Government or non government) during policy implementation. On the other hand, City Corporation is itself a hierarchic organization and consists of various departments. Hence, it requires ensuring sound coordination among all the departments within and out side RCC.

Practically ensuring sound coordination is a difficult task. It is very often seen that many policies remain stagnant in the half way mark due to lack of coordination among departments involved in carrying out these policies. Having this back ground in mind, I intended to identify causes of problems of coordination among various organizations and how it affects implementation of policies of urban governance in Bangladesh.

Moreover, the literature that analyze about the impact of problems of coordination in policy implementation of urban governance in Bangladesh is scanty. That is why, I am motivated to do this research and I hope this project would provide a new dimension to those academics and researchers who would like to continue research in the field of urban governance in Bangladesh in future.

RESEARCH OBJECTIVES

In the above discussion, it is indicated that problem of coordination has a negative impact on the implementation of urban policies in Bangladesh. To investigate why this happens during the implementation of policies one has to have a comprehensive understanding of the whole phenomenon. Therefore this study intends to address following issues:

(1) To explore problems of coordination among various agencies and departments within and outside the City Corporation involved in carrying out the policies of urban governance.

(2) To understand the existing relations among the city corporation and various central government departments and find out how these relationships affect the

implementation of policies of City Corporation which in the long run affect the quality of service provided to the citizens.

(3) To identify and explore the factors those impede coordination in the implementation of policies of urban governance.

RESEARCH QUESTIONS

In order to analyze the problems of coordination in policy implementation in the urban governance in Bangladesh the following questions need to be addressed:

(1) How is coordination achieved within City Corporation and among various organizations for the purpose of implementation of policies?

(2) Why problems of coordination (intra and inter) occurs in the policy implementation of urban governance?

(3) What impact intra organizational- coordination has on the implementation of policies of the urban governance?

(4) How inter-organizational coordination affects policy implementation of Urban Governance of Bangladesh?

SCOPE OF THE STUDY

The focus of the study is restricted to Rajshhai[5] City Corporation relating to the problems of coordination in the implementation of policies. The other part of the study is to explore how intra and inter organizational coordination affect policy implementation. Within the RCC, the implementation of the infrastructure policy is chosen as an area to examine the effects of coordination. Infrastructure policy here refers to those policies that initiate projects for the development of roads, bridges and water & sewerage within the RCC. In order to implement infrastructure policy, coordination with other government departments is required because of probing of resources, organizational and technical capacities.

RESEARCH DESIGN AND DATA COLLECTION

This study employs case oriented qualitative research strategy. A descriptive and exploratory case study approach was utilized for this policy study because how, what or why questions were posed, I had little control over the events, and the focus was on contemporary phenomenon (Yin, 1994, p. 1). In this regard, Rajshahi City Corporation has been selected for this study. The reason for the choice of case-study method is related to the problematic of this study, which is a complex issue. As Cresswell pointed out there are six assumptions in qualitative designs based on Merriam's (1988) assumptions, qualitative researchers are concerned primarily with (i) process, (ii) interested in meaning how people make sense of their lives, experience, (iii) the researcher is the primary instrument for data collection and analysis, (iv) it involves field work, (v) is descriptive in that the researchers is interested in process, meaning and understanding gained through words or pictures, (vi) qualitative research is inductive (Creswell 1994: 145, cited in Ahmed 2002:10). This strategy would likely to be appropriate for dealing with my research questions and objectives. I intend to study problems of coordination in the implementation process which requires understanding of relationships among different actors and organizations/ institutions involved in the implementation process.

Why Rajshahi City Corporation has been Selected?

In this study, the Rajshahi City Corporation has been selected among six City Corporations in Bangladesh for some reasons. *First,* the term manageability that often used for conducting social science research is one reason to choose Rajshahi City Corporation. *Second,* Rajshahi is the 4th largest city of Bangladesh with reasonable growth rate and a semi cosmopolitan nature. I have purposefully selected Rajshahi as an urban unit that may be representative of urban Bangladesh. Dhaka being the largest city of Bangladesh has lost its ability to represent the urban Bangladesh as a result of being the capital and having some other special historical features[6].

But Rajshahi has some similar characteristics[7] which are closer to other urban areas of Bangladesh. *Third,* I have selected Rajshahi as the field of study for personal reason. Rajshahi is a city where I have spent the last 13 years. I know the city to a great extent and have access to information. Having this consideration in mind, I liked to use my experience and network during the research work. Besides, it would be an intricate task for me to go to an unknown city for field study within the stipulated time of only two months.

Data Collection

This study is mainly based on qualitative data. However, some quantitative data were used, though limitedly, to supplement the qualitative data. In Creswell's term (1994:177) this can be termed as a dominant–less dominant design. The dominant design here is the qualitative design. Denzin (1978) (cited in Creswell 1994:174) used the term triangulation to argue for the combination of methodologies in the study of the same phenomenon. The concept of triangulation was based on the assumption that any bias inherent in particular data sources, investigators, and methods (Jick 1979, cited in Creswell 1994: 174, also cited in Karim 2000, 12).

The study has been conducted on the basis of primary as well as secondary data. Primary data relevant to the research objectives and questions has been collected through a structured interview guide having closed and open ended questions. During data collection, I used *four different types* of questionnaire. *One type* of questionnaire was used for the respondents belonged to the City Corporation, *another type* for the respondents who were in charge of various government departments at Rajshahi, *one type* for ward[8] commissioners, and *one type* for the general public. For collecting data regarding intra organization coordination, I interviewed[9] the Mayor and the administrative heads of different departments of the City Corporation. For gathering information about inter organization coordination, I interviewed the regional heads of various government offices[10] i.e., Roads and Highways Department (R&HD), Local Government Engineering Department (LGED) and Rajshahi Development Authority (RDA). Besides, I talked with few word commissioners and few general public[11] in order to be acquainted with the stakeholder's perception about the policy implementation and coordination. The following numbers of informants were interviewed:

Table 1
Categories of Respondents

City Corporation Officials	*Government Officials*	*Others*
	Rajshahi Development Authority (RDA)	
(1) Mayor	(1) Chairman	(10) Word Commissioners
(2) Chief Executive Officer	(2) Executive Engineer	(30) General Public
(3) Chief Executive Engineer	(3) Town Planner	
	Roads and Highways Department (R&HD)	
(4) Chief Medical Officer	(4) Executive Engineer	
(5) Budget Cum Accounts Officer	(5) Deputy Divisional Engineer	
	Local Government Engineering Department (LGED)	
(6) Public Relations Officer	(6) Executive Engineer	
	(7) Assistant Executive Engineer	
6	7	40

Secondary data has been gathered from Rajshahi City Corporation's general administration department and libraries, library of the department of Public Administration, Rajshahi University, library of the Center for Urban Studies (CUS), Dhaka, various published documents (articles, books, study reports etc.), news papers, unpublished thesis, research monographs and internet.

Problems of Data Collection

Conducting social research in developing countries is problematic and Bangladesh is not an exception. In my case, before starting data collection, the Mayor of Rajshahi City Corporation was approached and was kind enough to give an instant direction to his officials for whole hearted cooperation. However, contacting the Mayor was not an easy task since his contact was necessary to get access to other officials of the city corporation. But, the process of getting approval from the Mayor was a difficult task. Formal application was placed for the approval of the mayor in proper channel through the Chief Executive Officer (CEO). When the application was placed before him, he sent it to the secretary in charge of general administration who then marked and sent the application to the deputy secretary for proper action. The dilemma started at that time because the deputy secretary did not know how to proceed with the application and who would proceed. Finding no other alternative, the deputy secretary sent the application to the press and publication officer. In this way, more than one week passed, but no action was taken regarding the formal permission. At last it was possible for myself to meet the Mayor physically and laid before him another application on which he gave instant order. In true sense, the data collection started formally after the application being approved by the Mayor. Though it was possible to receive approval of the Mayor in the application, but I had to wait more than one and half months for his interview. Due to his work load and unavailability at Rajshahi, he was not available for formal interview. One may find contradiction between my experience during data collection and the statement which I made while arguing in favour of choosing RCC as study unit. The fact is that my confidence could not be upheld. I would not have realized this situation unless I acquired the practical knowledge. Once again, it has been proved that there is difference between assumption and practical situation.

When I approached one higher official of RCC with the questionnaire, the experience was bitter. At that time, the official was surrounded by few lower level officials. Having gone through the questionnaire, the official reacted negatively and refused to answer the questionnaire arguing that I was working as a spy of

Norwegian government. Norwegian government had given me lot of money for collecting information from Rajahahi City Corporation. The lower level officials who sat in front of the respondent expressed the same views and he (higher official) was quite silent. Efforts were then made to convince the official arguing that all the information would be used only for academic purposes and strict confidentiality would be maintained. Finally, he agreed to sit before me for interview. But he was very selective and answered few questions. The experience with the Chief Executive Engineer (CEE) was as frustrating as before. Day after day, he fixed the date of interview but did not speak. At last, I had to conduct interview in his residence at night. The same thing happened with other official heads of the city corporation. On the other hand, the experience in the government offices was much better than the City Corporation. Government officials were cooperative and showed willingness to speak on the issue under study.

Collecting secondary data from the City Corporation was also a matter of serious quandary. RCC does not maintain any data base. Even a brochure was not found in RCC which might illustrate overview information about the organization. I had to contact lower level staffs for collecting various documents.

Reliability of the Data

Punch (1998, cited in Haque, 2003: 10) argues that reliability is a central concept in measurement which means consistency. Consistency over time means whether similar results are expected over time given the same questionnaires and to similar group. This is in other words to ensure greater reliability so that a generalization is possible for a given phenomena. Whereas internal consistency relates to the findings to what extent they are in mutual agreement and not contradictory with one another.

With a view to ensuring reliability, questionnaires were formulated based on discussions with some key informants and by close inspection of the working environment of Rajshahi City

Corporation and other government departments. Close inspection was inevitable in order to acquire generalization regarding policy implementation and coordination. Key informants were selected from among the officials of RCC and various government departments who are involved with the implementation of infrastructure policy of RCC. Besides, a number of ward commissioners and a small number of stakeholders (general people) were also interviewed.

Validity of the Data

Validity is the strength of conclusions, inferences or propositions and as a concept very pertinent to the measurement criteria. Validity refers to the extent to which a measurement instrument (test, questionnaire, method, or technique) accurately measures what it is supposed to measure (Smith & Hunt 1997, retrieved from *http:/ www.utmb.edu/ dci/ JARGON/ RV.htm# Validity).* The problem of measurement, therefore, lies in the fact that whether there is the prevalence of lack of coordination? If it is evident, what are the causes and how it affects the policy implementation of urban governance in Bangladesh? While focusing on validity, officials from Rajshahi City Corporation and other governments department were targeted as respondents. Besides, few ward commissioners and few general public were also targeted as respondents in order to cross cheek the data. In order to ensure measurement validity, the questionnaires were administered personally with the respondents by having face to face conversation. As the data were collected through several questionnaires from different categories of respondents and various sources, they were triangulated so that the findings ensure internal validity and the accuracy of information matches with the reality.

ORGANIZATION OF THE THESIS

The thesis comprises of seven parts that are presented in seven chapters:

Chapter I is the introductory discussions that contains research problem, significance of the study, research objectives, research questions, research methodology and data collection strategies etc.

Chapter II is about the analytical framework of the study. It sheds light on the discussion and operationalization of dependent, intervening and independent variables and drawing of an analytical model for the study based on relationship of different variables.

Chapter III deals with the history and the present state of urban governance in Bangladesh highlighting the issue of coordination. Emphasis would be given to discuss whether structure or functions were given magnitude for the development of urban governance in Bangladesh.

Chapter IV consists of discussions regarding history, legal framework, policy subsystem, formulation and implementation process of policies and involved actors in the policy implementation of Rajshahi City Corporation. Efforts would be given to measure the extent of deviation that is found in operational stage of policy formulation and implementation of RCC based on empirical data.

Chapter V is the study of intra-organizational coordination. Specifically discussion would be made on how intra-organizational coordination affects policy implementation of Rajashahi City Corporation. In doing so, lack of institutionalized rules and regulations and financial management would be focused.

Chapter VI is also an analytical chapter based on data and observations. It sheds light on inter organizational coordination. The main concern of the chapter is whether inter-organizational coordination affects policy implementation of RCC or not. In order to analyze the issue of inter-organizational coordination, central-local relations and democratic versus bureaucratic accountability would be highlighted.

Chapter VII is the concluding chapter that highlights the major findings.

NOTES

1. Bangladesh is a South Asian country emerges as an independent state in 1971.

2. There are two types of institution in the Urban Governance in Bangladesh. For the divisional city, there are six City Corporations and for the urban areas (secondary towns), there are almost 279 Pouroshava.

3. Total territory of the Dhaka City Corporation, which is the largest City Corporation in Bangladesh.

4. Dhaka is the capital of Bangladesh.

5. Rajshahi is the one of six divisional cities in Bangladesh which is located 350 kilo meter north from the capital Dhaka. It is the fourth largest city in Bangladesh with a population of about 4 millions.

6. I made such comments because it is very difficult to compare Dhaka City Corporation with other city corporations in Bangladesh in any respect. From the point of view of the size of the territory, its financial ability and access to central government, Dhaka is superior to any other city corporations in Bangladesh. That is why, study on Dhaka City Corporation would not have been a proper representation of urban Bangladesh.

7. Characteristics include income generation, industrialization and rate of urbanization.

8. Word means territorial sub-units. RCC is divided in to thirty wards represented by thirty elected ward commissioners and ten women commissioners.

9. I interviewed the Mayor because he is the administrative head of the city corporation. I interviewed 10 commissioners among 40 commissioners who are involved with the implementation of various policy of RCC. But, I managed to interview only 10 commissioners among forty because they were either unavailable or were not willing to talk anything about the City Corporation. Besides, I interviewed chief of five departments who were involved in the implementation of the infrastructure policy of the Rajshahi City Corporation.

10. I interviewed the regional heads of the Roads and Highways Department (RHD), Local Government Engineering Department (LGED) and Rajshahi Development Authority (RDA) because these three departments were involved with the implementation of infrastructure policy of the Rajshahi City Corporation.
11. I talked with 30 general public with a view to knowing their perception about the development activities of the City Corporation. They were selected on random basis.

2

ANALYTICAL FRAMEWORK

INTRODUCTION

The main purpose of this chapter is to develop an analytical framework for describing and analyzing problem of coordination in the policy implementation in the urban governance of Bangladesh. In other way, the concern is to analyze the relationship of coordination and policy implementation in urban government bodies. For doing so, it is necessary to establish the relationship of the independent, intervening and dependent variables and to relate them with the broad theoretical perspectives.

DEPENDENT VARIABLE

Policy Implementation

A policy is a broad guideline of actions designed to achieve some objective(s) of goal(s). A policy can be transmitted into several programs or projects in order to realize the broader objectives as envisaged in the policy. It is said to be 'public' when it is concerned with public interest and formulated by legal government machinery. William Jenkins defines 'public policy' as a 'set of interrelated decisions taken by a political actor or group of actors concerning the selection of goals and the means of achieving them within a specified situation where those decisions should, in principle, be within the power of those to achieve'(Jenkins 1978, cited in Howlett and Ramesh, 1995:5). In fact, Jenkins views public policy as a process.

After a public problem has made its way to the policy agenda, various options have been proposed to resolve it, and a government has made some choice among those options, what remains is putting the decision into practice. This is the policy implementation stage of the policy cycle. The standard dictionary definition of the term implementation is simply, "to put into effect according to some definite plan or procedure" *(www.geocities.com/~profwork/pp/implement/define.html).*

McLaughlim (1985) defined implementation as 'the process whereby programs or policies are carried out; it denotes the translation of plans into practice' (quoted in Howlettt and Ramesh, 1995:153). According to Van Meter and Van Horn (1975), "policy implementation encompasses those actions by public and private individuals (or groups) that are directed at the achievement of objectives set forth in prior policy decisions". This includes both one- time efforts to transform decisions into operational terms, as well as continuing efforts to achieve the large and small changes mandated by policy decisions.

Focusing on the above discussion, we can draw a working definition of implementation as 'public policy implementation consists of organized activities by government directed toward the achievement of goals and objectives articulated in authorized policy statements'.

In the present study, discussion would be made on the implementation of policies of urban government bodies in Bangladesh. For this reason, Rajashahi City Corporation has been selected. However it is not possible to cover all the policies of RCC in a single case study. Therefore I would rather highlight the implementation of infrastructure policy of Rajshahi City Corporation. Implementation here is what happens after the infrastructure[1] policy is passed by the Corporation Parishad[2] of

RCC. The RCC authority faces a real challenge of maintaining coordination (both in terms of intra and inter-organizational coordination) when the policy comes in the implementation stage. The Engineering Department bears the responsibility of implementation of infrastructure policy. But, they require cooperation from other departments within City Corporation. On the other hand, they are to deal with various government departments working outside City Corporation. While dealing with different departments within and outside City Corporation, it is seen that total implementation process suffers from problems of coordination which foster delay in project completion, cost increase and unsatisfactory public service delivery. In this study, efforts have been made to analyze how lack of intra and inter-organizational coordination affect the implementation of infrastructure policy of RCC.

INTERVENING VARIABLE

Coordination

According to Shorter Oxford English Dictionary, Coordination means, 'the action of Co-coordinating; harmonious combination of agents and functions towards the production of a result' (Cited in Robinson, *et. al.* 2000:7). The most common notion of co-ordination is rule-regulated and hierarchically organized. This view of co-ordination has strong resonance with traditional views of management where the role of the manager is seen as being 'to plan, to organize, to command, to co-ordinate and to control (Fayol, 1916, cited in Robinson, *et. al.*, 2000:7). Co-ordination is a way to bring together disparate agencies to make their efforts more compatible (in the interests of equity, effectiveness and efficiency). Without co-ordination, the danger is of lapsing into chaos and efficiency.

In this study, co-ordination refers to working relationship among various departments and agencies within and outside the City Corporation that affect the implementation of policies in

Bangladesh. Coordination here is discussed in terms of intra and inter-organizational perspective.

Intra-Organizational Coordination

Mintzberg (1979) argues that when organization becomes complex, from simple to complex and from stable to dynamic, there is a need for different modes of intra-organizational coordination i.e., (i) Mutual Adjustment (ii) Direct Supervision (iii) Standardization of Work (iv) Standardization of Outputs (v) Standardization of Skills. *Mutual adjustment* achieves the coordination of work by the simple process of informal communication. *Direct supervision* achieves coordination by having one individual taking responsibility for the work of others. Work processes are *standardized* when the contents of the work are specified, or programmed. Outputs are *standardized* when the results of the work, for example the dimension of the product or the performance, are specified. Skills (and knowledge) are *standardized* when the kind of training required to perform the work is specified.

In the present study, the term intra-organizational coordination has been used to denote the existing working relationship among different departments within Rajshahi City Corporation. Sound working relationship has a long lasting impact on the over all policy implementation. But what happens when the question of lack of coordination within organization comes? The whole policy implementation process may be hampered.

Lack of intra-organizational coordination refers to the problematic working environment within the City Corporation which affects the policy implementation process. Lack of coordination takes place within organization when there is lack of communications, lack of rules, standard operating procedures and inadequate division of labour i.e., who will do what when and how? Actually, lack of intra-organizational coordination is a result of lack of institutionalization of settings of rules.

Lack of intra-organizational coordination always leaves negative impact on the overall policy implementation process. Here we can cite an example from the Dhaka City Corporation with a view to making our observation more valid:

> *Example*[3]
>
> The poor internal coordination in the DCC was glaringly brought out in its garbage disposal function. Owing to lack of understanding and cooperation between the Conservancy and Engineering Departments, tons of garbage remained piled up in Karwan Bazaar[4]. Indeed, if the DCC was effectively run, it could even sell this garbage since it is an excellent source of organic manure and purchase the pay loaders and the dumper trucks required for removing the garbage. Unfortunately, the two Departments were busy blaming one another while the garbage continued to pile up further. (The Daily Star, November 16, 1999, cited in Kamal Siddique *et.al.*, 2000: 85-86).

Lack of intra-organizational coordination has been used as intervening variables in this study. Rajshahi City Corporation is an autonomous organization although the government exercises extensive administrative and financial control over it. The nature of the organization is democratic,[5] on the one hand, and hierarchic,[6] on the other hand. While implementing the policies of the City Corporation, one department is interdependent with others within its framework. So, there is every possibility that problems of coordination may take place among them. In chapter 5, I would try to analyze how lack of intra-organizational coordination affects implementation of policies of Rajshahi City Corporation.

Inter-Organizational Coordination

When a policy is carried out by several organizations, inter-organizational coordination is important for the success of that policy. Inter-organizational coordination is manifested by the sound working relationship among the involved actors which is based on the rules and standard operating procedures. Van Meter and Van Horn (1975:465-67) wrote that effective implementation requires that a program's standards and objectives be understood by those individuals responsible for their achievement. Standards and objectives can not be carried out unless they are stated with sufficient clarity so that implementers can know what is expected of them. Communication within and between organizations is a complex and difficult process. If different sources of communication provide inconsistent interpretations of standards and objectives or if the same sources provide conflicting interpretations over time, implementors will find it even more difficult to carry out the intentions of policy.

However, it is not always possible to ensure effective communication among all involved parties. What happens when lack of inter-organizational coordination happens in the policy implementation due to lack of proper rules and regulations?

The most critical problem in urban governance in Bangladesh is the coordination among development partners, particularly in big cities, where the number of partner organizations is plenty and coordination is extremely important. For example, in Dhaka City, there are more than 16 government/autonomous organizations directly involved, and nearly 30 other organizations indirectly involved in urban development activities. Despite having an institutional arrangement for inter-organizational coordination among the first 16 bodies, real coordination has not yet been possible (Task Force on Urban Governance, 2001).

In this study, lack of inter-organizational coordination is also used as the intervening variables to measure its impact on the implementation of policies of Rajshahi City Corporation. While implementing the infrastructure policy, Rajshahi City Corporation deals with at least three government/autonomous departments who shares the responsibility of proving better infrastructure facilities to the citizens. These departments are Rajshahi Development Authority (RDA), Roads and Highways Department (R&HD) and Local Government Engineering Departments

(LGED). Lack of inter-organizational coordination means lack of communication between different agencies that leaves negative impact on the overall policy implementation process. The following example would prove the impact of lack of inter-organizational coordination:

> *Example: 1*
>
> In 2003, in Dhaka, the sufferings of the pedestrians and commuters using Mouchak[7] crossing of the city increased as the road between Mouchak and Malibagh[8] Railway crossing became almost unusable due to indiscriminate road digging by different utility agencies. Traffic jam in the area was worst than ever and sometimes it took hours to pass the crossing. The flooded road without any unusable pavements had worsened the situation to an intolerable level. The jam sometimes took more than hour to pass only this 300 to 400 yards road. The roads were submerged with water and full pot holes which often caused accidents.
>
> The news paper source said Dhaka Water and Sewerage Authority (DWASA) first cut the road for development works more than eight months ago but it was not repaired. The traffic congestion became worst when heavy rainfall lashed the city. Even residents of the area made a bamboo bridge on the road to cross from one side to other as knee-deep water remained stagnant for days. When contacted the authorities, one of the high official of DWASA told that the work was pending for last few months as they did not get the permission of the Railway authorities to cross DWASA line to the Malibagh rail gate. He also added that the work would be completed soon if they got the permission within short time.
> (The Independent, May 09, 2003).

The above example showed that due to lack of sound coordination among the Dhaka Water and Sewerage Authority (DWASA) and Railway, the road was kept unrepaired being dug eight months earlier. This caused intolerable sufferings to the general people. There are also plenty of other instances which would highlight problems of coordination between City Corporation and other government departments. A few are the followings:

Example: 2

The Dhaka City Corporation (DCC) builds and maintains roads and issues riskshaw[9] licenses, but motor vehicle licensing is the responsibility of the Bangladesh Road and Transport Authority (BRTA). On the other hand, the Dhaka Metropolitan Police (DMP) issues motor vehicle driver's licenses and manages city traffic and the Department of Environment monitors the emission of black gas by motor vehicles. These bodies are never known to sit across the table and learn about each other's difficulties (Siddique *et. al.* 2000: 196).

Example: 3

It is never known who is supposed to own and manage the manholes in a particular area of the Dhaka City, and there is a serious coordination problem in this regard between DCC and DWASA. Similarly, while surface drains are the responsibility of the DCC, the sewerage system is manned by DWASA, and owing to this dual administration, the two organizations constantly get away by blaming one another for the poor waste disposal in the City, while the citizens continue to suffer (Siddique *et.al.* 2000: 169).

All the above examples represent that the urban government bodies are to deal with different government and semi-government organizations in regard to the policy implementation. As a result of these interdependencies, problems of inter-organizational coordination may take place. Therefore efforts have been made here to analyze how lack of inter-organizational coordination affects the implementation of policies of Rajshahi City Corporation.

INDEPENDENT VARIABLES

Lack of Institutionalized Rules and Regulations

The proposition that organizations follow rules, that much of the behaviour in an organization is specified in the bureaucratic and organizational literature (March and Simon, 1958, cited in March and Olsen, 1989:21). It can be extended to the institutions of politics. Much of the behaviour in political institutions reflects the routine way in which people do what they are supposed to do. The rules may be imposed and enforced by direct coercion and political or organizational authority, or they may be part of a code of appropriate behaviour that is learned and internalized through socialization or education' (March and Olsen, 1989: 21-22).

According to March and Olsen (1989:22), "rules" are the routines, procedures, conventions, roles, strategies, organizational forms, and technologies around which political activity is constructed. They also mean the beliefs, paradigms, codes, cultures, and knowledge that surround, support, elaborate, and contradict those roles and routines. Routines are independent of the individual actors who carry them out and are competent of surviving substantial turnover in individuals. These routines may be procedural rules specifying a process that is to be followed under certain circumstances. They may be decision rules specifying how inputs are to be transformed into outputs. They may be assessment rules specifying criteria for evaluating results. Rules may standardize the distribution of authority and responsibility, record keeping, and information gathering and handling. They may spell out who has access to what institutions or arenas under which conditions, including the rights of political opposition. They may regulate the appropriate times for saying or doing things by providing deadlines or by imposing time period when certain things can not be said or done. They may regulate the changing of rules.

Based on the above theoretical explanation, it is clear that institutionalization of rules and regulations are important for cooperation among organizations. Rules decide who should do what, when and how? It allocates responsibilities, it divides functions between organizations and specifies the process of decision making. Rules structure coordination. In contrast, lack of rules breaks this structure and as a result line of command, functional responsibilities and .division of labour become ambiguous. Implementation suffers from a sense of direction and lack of commitment of who will do what and when. The coordination among various departments within an organization largely depends on the extent that the rules are clearly specified and everybody is well aware of his responsibility. The Rajshahi City Corporation is administered by the City Corporation Act, 1987 (Rajshahi City Corporation Act, 1987). But, this law has not been changed for the last 16 years. Besides, the laws are unclear in many respects. Because of the ambiguity they are quite often overlapping. These overlapping and improper uses of laws frustrate the officials that affect the intra-organizational relationship. The observation leads to the following hypothesis:

Hypothesis 1

The more structured the institutional rules and regulations in terms of who will do what and when, the less will be the coordination problems in policy implementation

Financial Management

It is widely alleged that the urban local bodies in the developing countries suffer from inadequate financial resources, not only for capital investment to meet the growing need of increasing urbanization, but even for continuation of the existing services. The case for urban governments in Bangladesh is equally true where these bodies have been persistently resource poor (Chowdhury, 1997: 27). The urban government bodies are empowered by the local government regulations to accumulate resources from local sources through assessment and levy of taxes, leasing of Hats[10] and Bazars[11], water bodies, etc.

The growth of urban population and demand for urban services has increased over the years but the capability of the cities to raise revenues has not improved considerably. Urban local government resources fall behind, infrastructure is poorly managed and services do not expand to cover new populace despite the overall augmentation of city wealth. As a result of insufficient services provided by the urban bodies, the people become even more hesitant to pay taxes that are a common problem for small, intermediate and large cities alike (Urban Edge 1984; World Bank; 1985, also cited in Chowdhury, 1997:27). The effect of the circumstances has pushed the hideous face of urbanization into sharp focus. There is almost a total collapse of urban services and this has resulted in lower urban efficiency and, in turn, lowers resources for urban government. This gave birth to inefficient financial management within the urban government bodies.

As the urban government bodies do not earn enough revenue from taxes and other sources, they depend on central government grants for financing development projects. But, the grants which they receive from the central government always fall behind their actual requirements. As a result of financial stress, City Corporation authorities face a difficult challenge of distributing these scarce resources among contesting demands and departments. In dealing with the distribution of funds, they can not satisfy all the departments which some times create intra-organizational coordination problems. The main concern here is to deal with financial management of the Rajshahi City Corporation and to find how it affects intra-organizational coordination that in the long run affects implementation of policies.

As City Corporation suffers from inadequate resources, managing financial affairs becomes difficult, especially distribution of resources among contesting departments. In such a situation, distribution of resources is made based on the strength of relationship of the departmental heads with the Mayor and powerful ward commissioners. This type of distribution criterion often frustrates other departmental heads which in the long run affects intra-organizational coordination. Based on these circumstances, the following hypothesis may be raised.

Hypothesis 2

The more the scarcity of financial resources, the more will be the problems of coordination.

Central-Local Relations

Governments exist at the national as well as at the sub national levels. The number and the structure of sub national governments depend upon the system of government adopted by a particular country in question. Generally, under a federal system, sub national governments exist at the state, provincial, and local levels, while under a unitary system, sub national governments exist at the local level only. (Jenkins, *et. al*, 2000: 1).

The most common way of describing central-local relation is based on central and local autonomy. On the one hand, the central is concerned with more control over local government and on the other hand, the local government is vying for more local autonomy. This tug of war is described in the following model.

Integrational and Autonomous Models

According to Francesco Kjellberg, changes in central-local government relationships can be analyzed from perspective of an 'autonomous model' or of an 'integrational model' (Kjellberg, 1995, cited in Montin and Erik, 2000:11). The autonomous model reflects the traditional liberal view of central-local government relationships. Central and local government constitutes in this perspective two clearly separated spheres of government where the state limits itself to monitoring the activities of local government. On the other hand, according to the integrational model, the relationship between central and local government is viewed as a question of functions, not as two separate political spheres. Local government participates in the entire social process, while any questions concerning who should be responsible for what should be decided from a pragmatic and flexible point of view (Montin and Erik, 2000:12).

The distinction between an autonomous and an integrational model reflects two sets of normative ideas on local government as to which should be the most important political institution within the framework of the constitutional state. The first model suggests that local government, because of its closeness to citizens and their problems and needs, should be highly autonomous. The second model suggests that the state is the sovereign political institution, but that it can invest different kinds of subordinated political institutions with delegated power. The clash of these two sets of ideas may be referred to as 'localism' versus 'integrationism'[12] (Montin and Erik, 2000:12).

Empirically, local self-government can mean different things depending on the perspective from which it is viewed. In the first perspective, it can be defined as a politically autonomous sphere with different characteristics which depend on the particular system of local government. Page (1991), for example, uses the concepts of 'legal localism' and 'political localism' in order to contrast different ways in which local government politicians can influence local decisions. The first broad method is to use their constitutional or legal status. The second is to use their political authority as democratically legitimated representatives of the locality (Page, 1991, cited in Montin and Erik, 2000:12). Another way of defining and measuring different types of autonomy is to use a 'resource perspective' in which local government has a greater or lesser degree of control over different critical resources, such as constitutional-legal, financial, political and professional controls (Rhodes, 1997; Elander & Montin, 1990, also cited in Montin and Erik, 2000:12). For example, local governments may have at their disposal a number of constitutional-legal resources, but they do not have the political, financial or professional resources for real policy-making (Montin and Erik, 2000:12). From an integrational perspective, local government can be described as a semi-autonomous political institution with a greater or lesser capacity for political action. It can be defined, for example, as a 'principal agency' or in terms of 'partnership' (Kjellberg, 1995). Other types of integration of central and local government which can be found in related literature are 'dual subordination' (the former soviet Union), 'dual supervision' (France), 'area subsidiarisation' (Germany) and 'functional regulation' (United Kingdom) (Montin and Erik, 2000:13).

It seems appropriate here to make a distinction between at least two situations of central-local government relations. In the first of these, local government is highly subordinated and local authorities may also be functionally divided into different policy sectors. In the second, central and local government relationships could be defined in terms of a partnership where there is a certain amount of room for negotiation and access to central state power. Local Government may depend on receiving resources from central government, but the state may in turn depend on local government to implement national policies (Sharpe, 1970). Central government may therefore be sensitive to pressure from local governments and their organizations.

In the context of Bangladesh, central-local relations have always been an issue. Here, statutorily, central-local relationship as provided in the statute has historically been authoritative in nature. This may be due to the colonial legacy and the absence of democratic government at the centre for a considerable period of time. The central or the national government primarily exercises its control over the urban local bodies through its field level government functionaries such as the Chief Executive Officer (CEO) and the Secretary in case of City Corporation, heads of various offices of district administration respectively those who are involved with the activities of the City Corporation. In addition, urban units are further controlled through a plethora of intricate and complicated orders and circulars from different agencies/

ministries which very often contradict the original legal framework. Under the law, again, the national government is also empowered to carry out inquiries into the affairs of urban local government institutions. And after such inquiry, if the government considers that a urban unit is 'unable' to discharge its duties; or 'failed' to meet its financial obligations; or otherwise exceeds or abuses its power, then the government may declare such bodies to be suspended for a period as may be specified by the law (Huq 2001,11-12).

In addition, the central government also exercises substantial financial and administrative control over the local government institutions in different ways. Especially in the case of allocation of resources. For the financing of the development projects, City Corporation has to depend fully on the central government grants. In the case of allocation of grants, it is very often seen the existence of 'ultra vires' power on the part of the central government. Allocation of grants depends on the existing relationship between the City Corporation and central government. Central government ignoring rules and norms, allocate more grants to the city corporation which is administered by the Mayor belonging to the ruling political party. On the other hand, City Corporation having the Mayor from the opposition suffers from various disparities twisted by central government. In such a situation, there is possibility of problems of coordination among these two organizations which in the long run affect policy implementation of City Corporation. Another factor that affects central-local relations is the contrast between autonomy and centralization. Local government bodies vie for more autonomy and central government tries to exert more control on local government bodies. This type of control also affects inter-organizational coordination that makes policy implementation problematic. Central-local relations do not only mean that the extent of autonomy central government allows to the local government or sum of resources central government allocates, this relationship takes different shape such as, access[13] of the local government bodies to the central government and geographical location[14]. Having this back ground, the following hypothesis may be drawn:

Hypothesis 3

The more the access to central-government, the lesser will be the problems of coordination in policy implementation.

Democratic versus Bureaucratic Accountability:

There is a sharp distinction between the City Corporation and various government departments with regard to their mode of operation and accountability patterns. City Corporations are political organs and popularly elected. Therefore, political leadership is responsible to the general public for every action. On the other hand, government departments are staffed by the civil servants who are accountable to their line ministries in a hierarchic manner. Wilson (1987) has rightly said that one of the important problems confronting the modern state is to identify a way to strike a balance between the politicians and the bureaucrat- the two contending elites in the policy process. Although the policy process is subject to influence and manipulation by a variety of individuals and institutions, these two sets of actors have nevertheless a special role to play (Cited in Ahmed, 2002:217). That is why, coordination among these two different organizations is indispensable[15] during the policy implementation.

We can call the City Corporation as a patrimonial[16] organization and government department as rational- legal system of public management (bureaucracy). Weber (1947) coined the phrase patrimonialism to describe situations where the administrative jurisdiction over certain domains, are given wide leeway regarding how to act. These measures are mostly informal or off the record.[17] Patrimonial administration is closely associated with clientelistic politics. Under a pure patrimonial system, an office is treated as a type of income-generating property, even of the sovereign can reclaim this property at will. Authority is thus decentralized, with incumbents typically free to decide exactly how to carry out their administrative responsibility (Brinkerhoff and Goldsmith, 2002:7). If we try to fit RCC with Weber's model of patrimonialism, it would be almost the same. The Mayor is the supreme authority of the RCC. As he is not capable of doing every thing, he has distributed many functions to his subordinate officials. There are no structured and well described laws. They are using and interpreting the old laws in accordance with their needs.

Weber contrasted patrimonialism with rational-legal system of public management, characterized by a graded hierarchy, written documentation, salaried, full-time staff and political neutrality. Reliable following of the official rules is highly valued in these systems. People working under them are not supposed to charge for services, except in the case of user fees, which go to the government not into the civil servant's pockets (Brinkerhoff and Goldsmith, 2002:7).

The basic difference between these two types of organization is based on the fact that patrimonial organization is rule of preference of one or several actor and rational legal organization is rule of law. Both are centralized and hierarchical. The former is centralized on the basis of tradition, family etc and the other is centralized on the basis of formal division of labour, functional units, etc. The Table 1 sums up the idealized distinctions between patrimonial and rational-legal bureaucratic system.

Although the urban governance bodies in Bangladesh are administered by people's representatives but they deal with various government offices administered by the bureaucrats who are working parallel within the City Corporation area. The basic contrast between the city corporation and the government agencies is based on their nature of accountability. The nature of the accountability of the City Corporation is bottom-up which refers that the City Corporation authorities are accountable to the people

Table 1
Continuum of Administrative Systems[18]

Patrimonial	*Rational-legal Bureaucratic*
• Administrators are recruited and promoted as reward for personal connections with political leaders.	• Administrators are recruited and promoted in competitive process that judge their merit and experitse.
• Administrators can be dismissed for no reason.	• Administrators can only be dismissed with cause.
• There is an unspoken hierarchy, with little specialization of specification of output and uncertain reporting channels.	• There is authorized hierarchy with clear division of labour, specific standards for output and well-defined reporting channels.
• Important orders may be given orally.	• Importing orders are put in writing.
• The public and private realms are blurred.	• The public and private realms are kept separate.
• Administrators supplement their salary with brides and . kickbacks	• Administrators are prohibiting from supplementing their salary.
• System is decentralized allowing wide discretion on the job.	• System is centralized with little room for discretion on the job.
• Administrator's action are arbitrary, based on subjective reasoning, and follow ad hoc procedures.	• Administrator's actions are predictable, based on objective methods, and follow uniform procedures.
• Rules are applied with partially and some citizens get . preferential treatment	• Rules are applied with neutrality and all citizens receive equal treatment.
• Verbal agreements are used in government procurement and sales.	• Binding legal contracts are used in government procurement and sales.
• Internal controls are relaxed.	• Internal controls are strict.
• Documentation is spotty with sensitive matters left off the books.	• Thorough records are maintained and regularly audited.
• Subjects have little recourse for poor service.	• Citizens have appeal channels if given poor service.

for their activities. The nature of accountability of the government agencies is top-down in which the officials are responsible to their higher officials. As the Mayor is the root of all powers, things can be done very fast within the City Corporation. But in the case of government offices, decision on any policy issues needs to be approved by the line ministries which take long time. When the question of inter-organizational correspondence comes, City Corporation expects speedy action from the government offices and wants thing to be done in their way. If government offices deny, problems of coordination occurs. Besides, the Mayor quite often tries to influence government offices. If officials disagree on issues where the Mayor actively participates, problems of coordination is seen which affect policy implementation. The following example provides an understanding about existence of ongoing contrast between democratic and bureaucratic organizations.

Example:

> In the Dhaka City Corporation Ordinance 1983, provision were made for inclusion of five top officials of Dhaka City, namely Chairman, RAJUK[19], Managing Director, DWASA[20], Chairman, DESA[21], Chief Engineer, DPHE[22] and Director General, Health Services as ex-officio Ward Commissioners with a view to making then as part of Corporation. It was based on the ideal for ensuring better coordination among the "core" services providers of Dhaka city. In practice, the initiative was failed, because most of these officials, out of bureaucratic vanity or departmental jealously, never turned up in the coordination meetings. (Siddique, *et. al,* 2000: 170-171).

The above observation may lead to the following hypothesis.

Hypothesis 4

The more the contrast between democratic versus bureaucratic accountability, the more will be the problems of coordination in policy implementation.

HYPOTHESES OF THE RESEARCH

Each study has its own specific purpose and it is designed accordingly. The design of this study is based on the urgency to acquire an understanding of how intra and inter organizational coordination affect the implementation of urban policies in Bangladesh. With a view to achieve an understanding of this issue, four hypotheses have already been drawn after the discussion of each independent variable. The following table shows them altogether.

Table 2
Hypotheses of the Research

Independent Variables	*Hypotheses*
Lack of Institutionalized Rules and Regulations	*Hypothesis 1:* The more structured the institutional rules and regulations in terms of who will do what and when, the less will be the coordination problems in policy implementation.
Financial Management	*Hypothesis 2:* The more the scarcity of financial resources, the more will be the problems of coordination.
Central-Local Relations	*Hypothesis 3:* The more the access to central-government, the lesser will be the problems of coordination in policy implementation.
Democratic versus Bureaucratic Accountability	*Hypothesis 4:* The more the contrast between democratic versus bureaucratic accountability, the more will be the problems of coordination in policy implementation.

CONCLUSION

My main intention is to analyze how lack of coordination affects the policy implementation of urban government in Bangladesh. In doing so, I tried to discuss the interrelationship among variables in the above discussion. Now I try to operationalize our analytical model based on the above discussions for presenting the study in a rational framework.

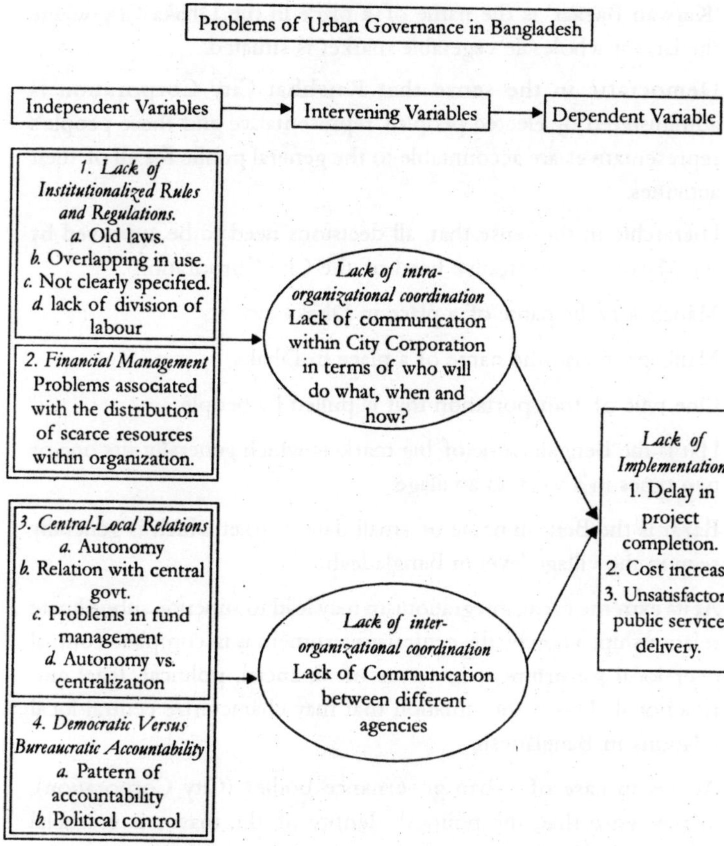

Figure 1 : *Conceptual Framework of the Study*

NOTES

1. Infrastructure policy refers to those projects which are initiated and implemented by RCC for development of roads, drains etc.
2. Corporation Parishad is the highest decision making of Rajshahi City Corporation.
3. Examples from Dhaka City Corporation are mostly mentioned in this chapter. Being located in the capital, Dhaka is well focused and highlighted by the Medias. Rajshahi as being located in the periphery, are not given much attention.

4. 'Karwan Bazaar' is the name of a place in the Dhaka City where the largest wholesale vegetable market is situated.
5. Democratic in the sense that Rajshhai City Corporation is administered by elected people's representative and these people's representatives are accountable to the general public for all of their activities.
6. Hierarchic in the sense that, all decisions need to be approved by the Mayor (administrative head of the City Corporation).
7. Mauchak is the name of a place in Dhaka city.
8. Malibagh is also the name of a place in Dhaka.
9. One type of transportation that is pulled by people.
10. Hat is the Bengali name of big markets which generally sits one or two times in a week in a village.
11. Bazar is the Bengali name of small daily market which is generally seen in the village level in Bangladesh.
12. At its extreme form, integrationism may lead to superior-subordinate relationship, whereby the central government is in complete control over local government in terms of financial, political, legal and functional. This is the situation that may characterize central-local relations in Bangladesh.
13. Access in case of urban governance bodies (City Corporation), in the sense that, the political identity of the mayor is a crucial factor. If the mayor of the city corporation belongs to the ruling party, he can enjoy more autonomy and financial wellbeing than that of a city corporation having mayor from opposition party.
14. Geographical location is also a crucial in case of central- local relations. The Dhaka City Corporation (situated in the Capital) is getting more benefits in every respect than other city corporations. Because, the Mayor of Dhaka City Corporation possesses good links with the central government.
15. One may ask why coordination is indispensable among these two organizations. We may find this answer in the words of Prud'home(1995). He rightly asserted that "Within a given

mega city, there are a frighteningly large number of actors, dimensions and concerns that have to be coordinated if the city is to function well and to develop harmoniously. There is no simple recipe for this formidable task" (Cited in Siddique, *et. al*, 2000:168).

16. Patrimonial in the sense that, City Corporation is headed by the Mayor. All power is vested in him. Nothing happens without his approval and he can do whatever he wishes. Nobody raises any protest against it.

17. Patrimonial rule has similarities to the feudal system of lord and vassal. Weber said the difference is that the feudal relationship is more ritualized and regularized, and thus more stable, than the ad hoc arrangements of patrimonialism.

18. Adapted from Brinkerhoff, W Derick and Arthur A Goldsmith, 2002:7-8.

19. RAJUK stands for Rajdhani Unnayan Kartripakkha (City Development Authority) which is entrusted with the responsibilities of preparation, implementation and monitoring of a master plan for Dhaka city.

20. Dhaka Water Supply and Sewerage Authority (DWASA) is the statutory body responsible for water supply, water-borne sewerage and sub-surface drainage in Dhaka city.

21. Dhaka Electricity Supply Authority (DESA) established on 1 October 1991 by a presidential ordinance. It works as an autonomous body and its objectives are to improve service of electricity to the consumers, improve transmission, and reduce system loss.

22. Department of Public Health Engineering (DPHE), a national agency under- the Ministry of Local Government Rural Development and Co-operatives is entrusted to provide safe water supply & sanitation and drainage facilities throughout the country except three major cities such as Dhaka, Narayanganj and Chittagong.

3

AN ACCOUNT OF THE DEVELOPMENT OF MUNICIPAL CORPORATION IN BANGLADESH HIGHLIGHTING THE ISSUE OF COORDINATION

INTRODUCTION

In order to understand the realities of lack of coordination in the urban governance bodies in Bangladesh, it is essential to have a clear idea about the development of urban government bodies. The purpose of this chapter is to give an account of the historical back ground of urban governance in Bangladesh and its present state of affairs highlighting the issue of coordination. Efforts are also made to analyze whether the development of the urban bodies were based on the structure or function?

THE EVOLUTION OF URBAN LOCAL GOVERNMENT:

Mughal Period: Dominance of Mir Mohallah

The development of the urban government system in the Indian subcontinent was first initiated by the Mughals (Siddique, 1994:33). During the Mughal period, importance the given to towns consisted of a number of well defined wards or mohallas. Mohalla was administered by a Mir Mahalla who represented the total population of that territory. Later on, the office of the Kotwal was developed as the keystone of the municipal organization during this period who was the chief executive of the town with extensive range of powers that includes magisterial, police and fiscal matters. Despite having these remarkable arrays of power, he had to perform a number of municipal functions where he was assisted by a judicial officer called Kazi and a Mohatasib in charge of preventing illegal matters (Siddique, 1992:17-18, cited in Khan, 1997:8-9).

However, urban government created by the Mughal suffered from lack of non-representativeness. There was no scope for the common people to express their opinions as it was a top-down administration and mainly an extension of central authority into the local areas. Under this system, it was a rule of hierarch when power was concentrated on the top. As a result, Mir Mahalla was the sources of all power and he gave decisions in all the matters. The emphasis was on structure and functional aspects were ignored and due emphasis was not given on matters regarding coordination.

British Period: Beginning of Representative Government

Careful, sluggish and steady progress was seen concerning the issue of urban local government institutions in the early ages of British rule. During those days, cities and towns grew up as centers of trade, industry and commerce, and as seats of government. By the enactment of the first Municipal Administration Act, 1793, municipal administration was established in the three presidency towns of Madras, Bombay and Calcutta. According to this law, Justice of peace was appointed by the government with a view to ensure the access to city houses and land, appointment of chowkidars[1], and to arrange scavenging and repair of roads in these cities (Siddique 1994, 43-44).

One visible fact was that, British officials or their nominated representatives dominated all the local government bodies during this period. In effect, the majority of the Indian population did not have the opportunity to express their views in the activities of these bodies (Khan, 1997:9). During the later part of their rule, the British passed number of laws for making the municipalities more representative to the general people of the Indian subcontinent. Consecutive laws introduced the means of election and extended its domain. But, provisions were also kept for the election of chairman and vice-chairman from among the commissioners. Bengal Municipal Act of 1932 was the first piece of municipal legislation in the region that widened and clarified powers of municipalities in levying rates and taxes and in the utilization of funds (Siddique 1994, 47). Simultaneously, unequivocal powers were given to government and local officers to inspect, supervise and control municipalities (Khan, 1997:9). Although, British government passed number of laws for establishing responsible urban government, but in actual practice, there was little scope for the general people to participate in the decision making process of urban government bodies. During the early days of Municipal administration, the British introduced the system of election based of restricted franchise. The electorate was only nine per cent of the total population and the voting rights depended on possession of property, income and qualifications. Voting was guided more by such considerations as kinship, group interests or communal affiliations than general welfare of city dwellers. During these days, election turned into a contest of wealthy, ambitious and selfish individuals whose interest lay in enhancing their self-interest often using thugs and musclemen to that end. As a result, internal dispute, jealousy, enmity, revenge and personal aggrandizement came to be synonymous with the municipality (Ahmed 1991, 151-182, cited in Khan, 1997:9). Khanum (1991) argued that due to lack of available financing, basic amenities provided by the Dhaka Municipality between 1920s and 1940s were inadequate and inefficient. Even the minimum mandated functions were financed by government grants as its resource base was narrow. No serious initiative was taken on the part of the municipality to raise additional taxes. The estimated income was also not collected. As a result, the supply and maintenance of basic services were affected. During this period, local patronage and the maintenance of a traditional power structure were the deciding factors of the politics of the municipalities which lacked vision to develop and provide basic amenities to all citizens (Khan 1997:10-11).

Based on above discussion, it is obvious that during the British Period, urban governance meant urban government. The same type of government created by the Mughals continued during the British Period with minor changes. The municipal government was the main body whose main function was law and order control and restoration. Since development activities were limited, these were mainly carried out by the municipal government and there was no other specialized body in charge of specialized function. As a result, coordination was not an issue. The main concern was to create a local body which carried out the directives of the colonial power.

Pakistan Period: Representative Government under the Veil of Authoritarianism

The Pakistan government continued the same urban local government system that was existent in the British India during their first ten years rule. Later on, some important changes were brought about by the then provincial government relating to local government (both urban and local) bodies in the province. The enactment of the new Municipal Administration Ordinance, 1960 was to bring the Municipalities in line with the so-called Basic Democracies[2] institutions in rural areas (Siddique, 1994:54). Municipal committees, town committees, union committees and ward committees were constituted to become components of the 'new' urban local government system. But these committees suffered from a variety structural and other deficiencies. Municipal committees, formed to run the municipalities, lacked representative character as chairmen and half of the members were officials (Khan, 1994a). The town committee was small municipalities. These consisted of elected members who in turn elected one of them as chairmen (Siddique, 1994:55). Both union and ward committee members included elected and appointed members. The exact nature of responsibilities of union committees was not clear. The ward committees were given a few ordinary functions. The sources of finance of these bodies expecting governmental grant were also not specified. In true sense, the concept of Basic Democracy, a four-tier system, lacked novelty and innovation. It bore a clear resemblance of two layers, the union councils and municipal committees of the British days (Khan 1997:11).

Based on the above discussion, it is clear that, laws regarding the development of urban bodies during this period were unclear in many respects. There was no division of responsibilities among different committees. While in operation, which committee would do what and how, was a matter of serious concern that very often gave birth to conflicting situation.

Bangladesh Period: Process of Experimentation

Since Independence in 1971, a number of attempts have been made to experiment with the urban-local government system in Bangladesh. Changes have been made from time to time in terms of the nomenclature of tiers of local government, but almost nothing was done to strengthen urban-local governments. Therefore, the structure of the urban-local government system has remained more or less unchanged.

Immediately after Independence in 1971, the name of the Union Council was changed to Union *Panchayat* and an administrator was appointed to manage the affairs of the *Panchayat.* The name of *Thana* Council was changed to *Thana* Development Committee while the District Council was named *Zila* Board or District Board. Again in 1973, Union *Panchayat's* name reverted to Union *Parishad.* A more significant change in the local government system was brought about in 1976 through the Local Government Ordinance. This ordinance provided for a Union *Parishad* for a union, a *Thana Parishad* for a *Thana* and a *Zila Parishad* for a district. The Union *Parishad* comprised one elected Chairman and 9 elected members, two nominated women members and two peasant representative members. The *Thana Parishad* consisted of the Sub-Divisional Officer being the ex-officio Chairman, the Circle Officer and a Union *Parishad* Chairman. The *Zila* (District) *Parishad* was to consist of elected members, official members and women members whose numbers were determined by the government. Its term of office was five years. However, no elections were held and government officials ran the *Parishad (http://www.unescap.org/huset/lgstudy/country/bangladesh/bangladesh.html#ahead).*

In 1980, as a result of an amendment of the Local Government Ordinance, the *Swanirvar Gram Sarker* (self-reliant village government) was introduced at the village level, but was abolished by a Martial Law Order in July 1982. A major change was initiated in the local government system through the introduction of the Local *Government (Upazila Parishad* and *Upazila* Administration Reorganization) Ordinance in 1982. This Ordinance was followed by the Local Government (Union *Parishad*) Ordinance in 1983, the Local Government (*Zila Parishad*) Act in 1988 and the three Hill Districts Acts and *Palli* Act in 1989. The *Upazila Parishad* Ordinance (1982) was particularly significant as this was supposed to help implementation of the decentralization programme of the government. In the *Upazila* System (as it came to be known), the (directly) elected Chairman would have the principal authority in running the affairs of the *Upazila*, his tenure being five years. The *Upazila Nirbahi* Officer (UNO) would be subservient to the Chairman. After nine years of reasonably effective implementation, the Government of the Bangladesh Nationalist Party, who came to power through a fair election, abolished the *Upazila* system in 1991. During its five-year tenure, the government could not provide an alternative democratic form of local government. When after another free and fair election in 1996 the Bangladesh Awami League came to power, they constituted a Local Government Commission and came up with a Report on Local Government Institutions Strengthening in May 1997. The Commission recommended a four-tier local government structure including *Gram/Palli* (Village) *Parishad*, Union *Parishad*,

Thana/ Upazila Parishad and *Zila* (District) *Parishad*. The present government after caming into power in 2001 initiated a change in the local government structure. The have introduced Gram Sarker (GS) in place of Gran Parishad. Recently, an Act was passed for the creation of Gram Sarkars. These bodies have been created at the Ward levels. Each Gram Sarker represents 1-2 villages comprising of about 3,000 people on an average. The UP member elected from the Ward Chairs the GS, which consists of other members, both males and females, elected in a general meeting of the voters of the Ward under the supervision of a 'prescribed/ directing authority'. There are defined functions of the GS and other functions may be assigned to it as may be specified by the government from time to time. GSs have the right to constitute issue-based standing committees as and when required, and to determine the membership of such committees.

All these tiers are concerned with rural/regional administration, while urban local governments remain outside the Commission's purview. The two major tiers of urban local government's, *Pourashava* (for smaller Municipalities) and City Corporation (for the six of the largest cities) are in order.

Local Government Categories and Hierarchies in Bangladesh

The rural/regional local government as proposed by the latest commission on local government would have four tiers:

(1) *Gram* (Village) *Sarkar*

(2) Union *Parishads* (4403);

(3) *Thana/ Upazila Parishads* (460);

(4) *Zila* (District) *Parishads* (64).

Urban areas have a separate set of local governments. The Bangladesh Census Commission recognized 522 urban areas in 1991 (with a population of about 5000 or more) but only about 279 of the larger urban areas among these have urban local governments. The Six largest cities have a City Corporation status, while the rest are known as *Pourashavas* or Municipalities, which again are classified according to financial strength.

Table 1
Hierarchy of Urban Local Governments[3] in Bangladesh

City Corporation	*Dhaka, Chittagong, Khulna Rajshahi, Borishal and Syllehet*
Pourashavas (Municipalities)	279
Category	Annual income level[4]
Class I *Pourashavas*	6 million +
Class II *Pourashavas*	2 million
Class III *Pourashavas*	Less than 2.5 million

In addition, there are also some urban centers that are under military Cantonment Boards. The City Corporation and *Pourashavas* (Municipalities) are true urban local governments. The large number of small urban centers is administered under the Union *Parishad* system of (rural) local government. Some urban centers have a fairly large population but have not yet been' declared a Municipality and therefore also remain under Union *Parishad* management. The existing structure of the urban-local bodies in Bangladesh can be shown by the Figure 1.

The foregoing discussion has made it clear that, after the independence of Bangladesh, every successive government tried to change the structural aspect of the urban local government bodies ignoring the importance of functional aspects. In doing so, they have introduced several changes in the urban-local government system. Actually, they have overlooked the fact that structure can not work unless the functions are clearly specified. As a result of this, every unit of the urban-local government bodies suffer from problems of coordination in their operation.

COORDINATION AMONG URBAN-LOCAL GOVERNMENT BODIES IN BANGLADESH

The essence of coordination among different urban-local bodies is unquestionable. Siddiqe (1994:304-305) argued that coordination

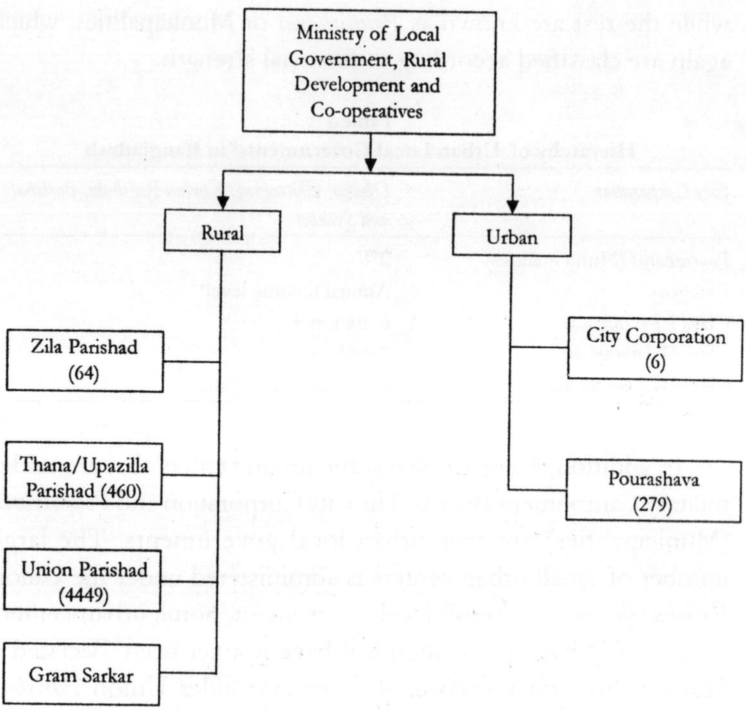

Figure[5] 1: *Existing Structure of Local Government in Bangladesh*

/cooperation among different urban-local bodies is important for several reasons. *First,* it could pave the way for the identification and solution of common problems. *Second,* it could lead to pooling and sharing of costly machinery, scarce financial resources, expertise and experience for providing certain common services in respect of public health, planning, election administration, staff training public works, tax assessment and collection, waste disposal, recreational facilities, civil defense, etc. *Third,* coordination/ cooperation among local government bodies could not only help resolving disputes without outside intervention but also engender joint venture projects. *Fourth,* it could also be utilized for standardizing services, work procedures, personnel systems etc. *Finally,* it is only through getting together that local government bodies can challenge their existing peripheral status and strike a better deal with the national government.

At present there are hardly any formal or informal arrangements for coordination/cooperation among urban local government bodies at the same level. In fact, it is only during training programmes or conventions arranged by the national government that functionaries of local government are able to come together and get to know each other's problem to some extent. However, such get together are few and far between (Siddique, 1994: 305). In the case of City Corporation, in 1996, after Awami League (AL) came into power established a high power coordination committee in each City Corporation chaired by the minister in charge of local government, rural development and cooperatives (LGRD&C) of which the Mayor acted as the co-chairman. Top official of various service providing institutions[6] were also included as the members. The committee was formed in order to ensure better management of services within the territory of the City Corporation and to settle disputes among City Corporation and various government agencies. Although the Committees were formed, controversies were going on regarding effectiveness of this Committee. Siddique et,al (2000: 171) in their studies found that the coordination committee which was formed in Dhaka City Corporation were not quite effective in settling matters of dispute. They asserted that:

> "From 1996 to late of 1998, the coordination committee of DCC had met 11 times in order to settle matters of dispute, but they succeeded in one case. The only outcome of these deliberations was some progress in dealing with water logging and mosquito control in Dhaka city. Discussions were also made on traffic management and garbage disposal, but were not resulted in any concrete decision".

During this period, there was little scope to take the initiative for settling matters of disputes. But, Bangladesh Nationalist Party (BNP) after coming to power in 2001 stooped the operation of this coordination committee. Now there is no coordinating body in the urban governance that may deal with matters of dispute.

CONSTITUTIONAL AND LEGAL BASIS OF URBAN LOCAL GOVERNMENT IN BANGLADESH

In a democratic country, Constitution ensures the legal recognition of the local government by an act of the parliament or incorporating relevant provisions (Khan, 1997:11). The legal basis and responsibilities of the local government in Bangladesh is clearly spelt out in the Constitution of 1972. The article fifty-nine of chapter three of the Constitution stated that, 'Local government in every administrative unit of the Republic shall be entrusted to bodies composed of persons elected in accordance with law". Article sixty of the Constitution states 'for the purpose of giving full effect to the provision of article fifty nine, Parliament shall, by law, confer powers on the local government bodies referred to in that article including power to impose taxes for local purposes, to prepare their budgets and to maintain funds (Constitution of The People's Republic of Bangladesh, 1991:43).

In this section it is necessary to mention about the constitutional and legal basis of the local government of Bangladesh because if the duties and responsibilities of the urban/ local government institutions are not demarcated by the Constitution or by the act of the parliament, or if there is no scope for the people to be elected in the urban/local bodies, then it is difficult to ensure people's participation. From the above discussion, it is evident that the legal basis of the local government is clearly spelt out in the Constitution and the Constitution by the article fifty nine of the chapter three has ensured the scope for the people to be elected in the local government bodies.

INSTITUTIONAL FRAMEWORK OF URBAN GOVERNANCE OF BANGLADESH

Some institutions that are involved in the service delivery of urban governance in Bangladesh have been classified under four broad headings (Chowdhury, 1989, 1994 cited in Khan, 1997:13). These four categories included: (i) municipal government, (ii) special development bodies, (iii) special purpose authority and (iv) special government bodies. The classification schema is relevant for our purpose because it covers all types of organizations that are involved in urban governance. Hence, it needs further elaboration.

Municipal Government

Municipal government includes municipal corporations and pourshavas or municipalities. Currently, there are six municipal corporations-one each at Dhaka, Cittagong, Rajshahi, Khulna, Sylhet and Barisal and two hundred seventy nine pourashavas spread all over the country. All the municipal corporations and municipalities are run by a number of ordinances and acts that have been amended from time to time. The chairmen and commissioners of pourashaves, mayor and commissioners of municipal corporations and women member in both the cases in the reserved seats are directly elected on the basis of adult franchise. All the municipal corporations include a certain number of official commissioners designated by the government who are topmost functionaries of special development bodies, special purpose authority and special government bodies. Parliament passed several statutes for the creation of pourashaves and city corporations in order to serving the inhabitants of small and medium cities and metropolitan cities respectively. The chartered functions of both the urban local government institutions are remarkably similar that includes fifteen compulsory and thirteen optional functions. But it has been found that both these urban local bodies can not execute all the mandated functions due to number of reasons like, shortage of funds, poor and irregular collection of taxes, non-realization of taxes from government, semi-autonomous and autonomous offices for years together etc (Siddique, 1994: 146). City corporation and pourashavas extend municipal services ranging from construction of roads, bridges, culverts; removal, collection and disposal of refuse, wastes, rubbish; provision of water supply; provision and maintenance of street lighting; registration of births; marriages and deaths, provision and maintenance of graveyards and cremation grounds; eradication of mosquitoes; issuance of different kinds of certificates and provision to maintenance of parks and gardens (Siddique, 1994: 146-147).

Special Development Authorities

Four Special Development Authorities for four City Corporation have been created in Bangladesh for the purpose of providing with urban planning activities pertaining to infrastructure and site development activities for housing, commercial and industrial use. These four Special Development Authorities are Rajdhani Unnayan Kortipokkho (Capital Development Authority)-RAJUK for Dhaka City Corporation, Chittagong Development Authority (CDA), Khulna Development Authority (KDA) and Rajshahi Development Authority (RDA). These are semi-autonomous and autonomous bodies and run by chairmen and boards. Most members of these boards are government officials. Hence these boards lack representative character in terms of the communities served which reduce their accountability and consequently their credibility and public support (UNDP/HABITAT, 1992:9, cited in Islam and Khan, 1997: 14). Due to inadequate management and financial system, multiplicity of institutions having urban development functions within their jurisdiction, uncoordinated development, lack of interactions with other agencies, inadequate manpower and lack of people's participation, these authorities have not been effective in discharging their assigned duties and responsibilities (The World Bank, 1981; Mohit, 1992). A study on RAJUK found a number of problems related to the culture of organization. These problems included, unwillingness to change, difficulty of exerting the power of leadership, absence of customer/client orientation, factionalism, low image among other organizations involve in metropolitan management system, lack of integrity and lack of incentives (UNDP/HABITAT, 1992: 11-12, cited in Khan, 1997: 14).

Special Purpose Authority

Two organizations have been created by the government with a view to providing with the construction, improvement, expansion and maintenance of water and sewerage services. The organizations are Dhaka Water and Swerage Authority (DWASA) and Chittagong Water and Swerage Authority (CWASA). These organizations are run by chairmen and board members who are government officials.

Special Government Bodies

There are several Special Government Bodies that are working in the urban areas. These are fully government organization those have country–wide focus, but still their activities are primarily confined to urban bodies. Public Works Department (PWD) is responsible for constructing government offices and public buildings and works under the Ministry of Public Works and Housing (MPWH). It mostly undertakes construction of buildings in urban areas. Power and Water development Board (PWDB) works under the Ministry of Energy and responsible for generation and distribution of electricity throughout the country. The pourashavas and the City Corporations are required to provide limited infrastructure to facilitate the distribution of electricity in their jurisdiction. Urban Development Directorate (UDD) is the main government agency concerned with the physical development of the country. It is also responsible for preparing and coordinating regional plans and master plans for urban areas excepting four metropolitan cities, advising government on policies relating to land use and land development. It works also under the MPHW. The Department of Public Health and Engineering (DPHE) is responsible foe development of water supply and sanitation in rural and urban areas excepting in cities, like Dhaka and Chittagong. It is headed by a chief engineer and falls within the jurisdiction of the Ministry of Local Government Rural Development and Cooperatives (MLGRD&C). The Local Government Engineering Department (LGED) that works under the MLGRD&C is responsible for low-cost sanitation, infrastructure and improving physical environment (Khan. 1997:15).

CONCLUSION

Urban Local government as a political institution to ensure public participation in development activities is yet to take proper shape in Bangladesh. Since Independence in 1971, successive governments tried to make structural changes in the urban-local government system ignoring their functional implication. That is why, all most all the local government bodies suffer from various problems. In City Corporation area, there are several government organizations working along with them to provide better urban service to the citizenry. But, how their work would be coordinated, has not been specified in any where, or there is hardly any coordinating body. That is why, there always remains a question of inter organizational coordination and cooperation while discharging the duties and responsibilities of both urban government bodies and government organizations as they are to deal with each other in many respects.

NOTES

1. 'Chowkidar' means village watchman.
2. The military ruler which staged a coup d'etat in 1958 used to believe that the intellect of the Pakistani people was not suited to the Westminster-type representative government. The new regime was in favour of a guided democracy, which was to be characterized by authoritarian government at the top and representative government at the local level. This variety of local government was known as 'Basic Democracy' (Siddique, 1994: 48).
3. The table is made by the author based on information collected from *http://www.unescap.org/huset/lgstudy/country/bangladesh/bangladesh.html#* ahead and various news paper sources.

4. The Pourashavas has been classified in three categories depending on the extent of their annual income.
5. The figure has been drawn by author based on Siddique, 1994: 325 and *http://www.unescap.org/huset/lgstudy/country/bangladesh/bangladesh.html#ahead.*
6. Inclusion of higher officials from different service providing institutions in to the coordination committee varied depending of the City Corporation. In case of Dhaka City Corporation, top officials from Rajdhani Unnayan Kartripakkha (RAJUK), Dhaka Water Supply and Sewerage Authority (DWASA), Dhaka Electricity Supply Authority (DESA), Department of Public Health Engineering (DPHE), Power Development Board (PDB), Bangladesh Telephone and telegraph Board (BTTB) etc. were included as members. In case of RCC, top officials from Rajshahi Development Authority (RDA), Roads and Highways department (R&HD), Local Government Engineering Department (LGED), Bangladesh Telephone and Telegraph Board (BTTB) were included in the coordination committee as members.

4

Rajshahi City Corporation: Involved Actors in the Process of Formulation and Implementation of Policies

INTRODUCTION

The purposes of this chapter are two-fold. First, it explores the structural and functional aspect of the Rajshhai City Corporation (RCC) highlighting legal matters. Second, it analyses the formulation and implementation of polices of RCC, specially the infrastructure policy. In doing so, this chapter analyses the policy subsystem, policy making and policy implementation process of RCC. At the same time, this chapter focuses attention on the activities of those government departments that are involved in providing urban infrastructure services within RCC. Besides, efforts are made to highlight the extent of their linkage to RCC.

ORIGIN OF RAJSHAHI CITY CORPORATION

Rajshahi City Corporation started its activities in 1st of April, 1876 as Rajshahi Pourashava. Rajshahi Pourashava was administered by eight members town committee headed by the then Rajshahi College Principal. All the members were nominated by the government. The district magistrate, sub-divisional chief and the chief medical officer were the members of the town committee by virtue of their positions. Later on, provision was made for the election of chairman and vice-chairman by vote of the tax payers within the jurisdiction of the Pourashava. In 1884, a committee was formed comprising twenty one commissioners. Among them fourteen were elected and seven were nominated. For the effective delivery of urban services, eight urban committees were formed in 1930 and were responsible for administration, finance, man power, light, water, sanitation, health and education. Decisions were taken in the parishad meeting based on the recommendations of the various committees. Each committee was formed for one year term and the whole urban area was divided in seven wards. In 5th august 1958, dissolving the municipal committees, the government appointed administrator for Rajshahi Pourashava. Till 18th February, 1974, government officials acted as the administrator. On 13 August 1987, Rajshahi Pourashava was upgraded to Pour Corporation and on 11 September of the same year, Pour Corporation was changed to City Corporation. The first Mayoral election of RCC was held in 30th of January 1994.

LEGAL FRAMEWORK, COMPOSITION AND STRUCTURE OF RCC

The present legal framework of the RCC is provided by the Rajshahi City Corporation Ordinance, 1987 and subsequent amendments. Apart from these, there are other rules, bye-laws, regulations and standing orders. In practice, the government simply adapted the existing Pourashava rules for the RCC. These are concerned with personnel, finance, contracts, elections, inspection, property, etc. relating to the RCC. Over the years number of criticism had been made regarding the RCC's legal framework. *First,* most of the rules, regulations and bye-laws came into force a long time ago, and hence many of these have lost their operational value with the passage of time. In framing either the main law or the rules there under, the government undertook no meaningful consultation with either the RCC or outside experts. *Second,* some of these, with political overtones, have been subject to frequent amendments for political convenience. *Third,* standing orders are basically executive decisions, and to allow the central government to use these even when it has two other legal instruments at its disposal to deal with the RCC does not make any sense. *Fourth,* the DCC does not possess the legal expertise to either creatively amend the existing bye-laws and regulations or make new ones.

Under the Rajshahi City Corporation Ordinance, 1987, total area under the corporation is divided into 30 wards to elect 30 wards commissioners and 10 women commissioners (one third of the commissioners). The RCC is headed by Mayor who is directly elected by the people. As head of the corporation, all powers rest with the Mayor. It is entirely up to the Mayor to decide how much of what he will delegate to the lower levels. He can also overrule the decisions taken in the Corporation meetings. The RCC is required to form 11 standing committees to deal with the following subjects:

Finance and Establishment

Education

Health, Family Planning and Sanitation

Town Planning and Improvement

Audits and Accounts

Works and Buildings

Water

Electricity

Social Welfare and Community Centers

Transportation

Women and Children.

With the prior approval of the government, the Corporation may also constitute additional Standing Committees for such purposes, as it thinks fit. A Standing Committee is to consist of not more than six members, elected by the commissioners from among themselves. No commissioner is allowed to be the member of more than two Standing Committees at the same time. However, the Mayor is to be member of all the standing committees. A standing Committee is to elect one of its members as chairman and another as vice chairman. Besides, the concerned department head acts as the member secretary of each Standing Committee.

All the decisions are taken in the Corporation Parishad[1] which is composed of Mayor and forty word commissioners. The Corporation must hold meeting at least once in a month. Its meeting is presided over by Mayor and in absence of Mayor, a commissioner to be elected from among the members present for this purpose. Meeting is to be conveyed by Mayor at any time but in case they receive a written request from two third majority commissioner to hold meeting they are bound to call it. No business can be done unless there is quorum which consists of one third of the total members present, and all decisions must carry the support of majority members present in the meeting. All members have one vote each and only in case of tie the chairman exercises his casting vote (Rahman, 1989: 168).

For carrying out the activities of RCC, it is divided into six administrative departments. These departments are secretarial department, accounts department, revenue department, works department, sewerage department and public health department. Under each department, there are various branches. The composition and structure of RCC may be shown by the following figure.

FUNCTIONS OF RCC

The detailed functions of the RCC have been clearly spelt out in Part IV of the Ordinance. The functions of RCC have been categorized as 'compulsory' and 'optional' but the functions have not been listed under the heading of each category. For distinction of such functions the use of the term 'shall' and for some functions and 'may' for other in the Ordinance may be taken as a criterion.

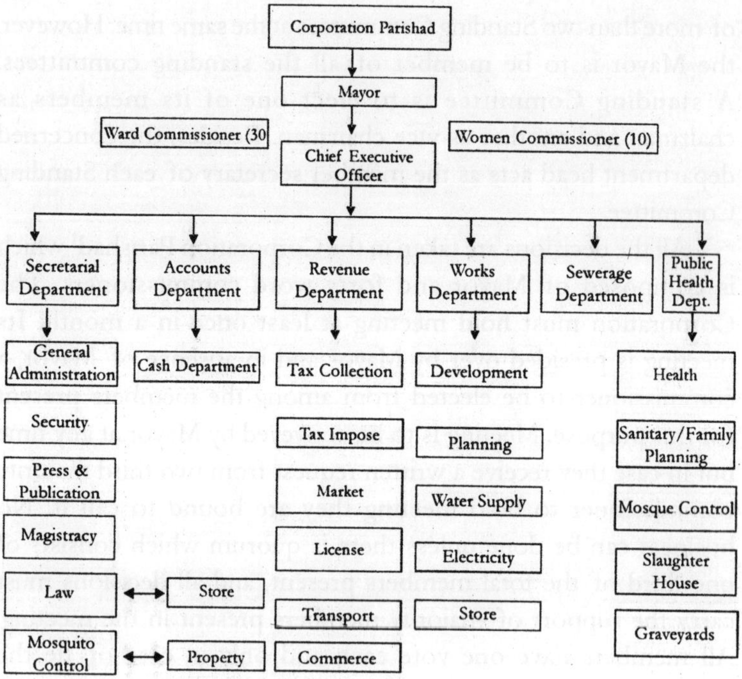

Figure[2] 1 : ***Composition and Structure of*** *RCCG*

Compulsory Functions

The compulsory functions of the RCC are the following:

(1) Construction and maintenance of roads, brides and culverts;

(2) Removal, collection and disposal of refuse, wastes and rubbish;

(3) Provision and maintenance of streets light.

(4) Maintenance of public streets and provision of watering them.

(5) Provision and regulation of water supply;

(6) Construction and maintenance of public markets/ shopping centers;

(7) Plantation of trees on the road sides;

(8) Regulation of in sanitary building;
(9) Preventions of infectious diseases and epidemics;
(10) Registration of births, deaths and marriages;
(11) Provision and maintenance of slaughter houses;
(12) Provision and maintenance of drainage;
(13) Control over erection and re-erection of buildings;
(14) Provision and maintenance of graveyards and cremation grounds; and
(15) Control over traffic and public vehicles.

Optional Functions

The optional functions of the RCC are as follows:

(1) Checking adulteration of foods and drinks;
(2) Control over private markets and shopping centers;
(3) Maintenance of educational institutions and provision of stipends to meritorious students;
(4) Provision of floods and famine relief;
(5) Provision and maintenance of parks, gardens and playgrounds;
(6) Establishment of welfare homes, orphanages and prevention of beggary;
(7) Establishment of public dispensaries;
(8) Provision of public toilets;
(9) Establishment of veterinary hospitals;
(10) Registration of cattle sales and, improvement of livestock;
(11) Celebration of national holidays;
(12) Reception of distinguished visitors/persons;
(13) Establishment of public libraries and reading rooms;
(14) Promotion of community development schemes; and
(15) Naming of roads and numbering of houses.

Functions Actually Performed

In theory, the City Corporations are empowered to perform a wide range of functions as described above. In practice, they are not able to do so mainly due to acute shortage of funds caused by poor collection of taxes, non-realization of taxes from Government and semi-government establishments for year's together and insufficient grants from the Central Government (Murtaza, 2002: 29). However, at present, the functions of the RCC are limited to the following:

(1) Construction and maintenance of roads, bridge, culverts, etc.;

(2) Removal, collection and disposal of refuse, waste and rubbish;

(3) Provision and maintenance of street lights;

(4) Provision of water supply;

(5) Construction and maintenance of public markets and shopping centers;

(6) Eradication of mosquitoes;

(7) Registration of births, deaths and marriages;

(8) Provision and maintenance of slaughter houses;

(9) Provision and maintenance of drainage;

(10) Naming of roads and numbering of houses;

(11) Provision of public toilets; and

(12) Provision and maintenance of parks and gardens.

POLICY SUBSYSTEM OF RCC: INVOLVED ACTORS IN THE POLICY MAKING PROCESS

Policies are made by policy subsystem consisting of actors dealing with a public problem. The term 'actor' includes both state and societal actors, some of whom are intimately involved in the policy process while others are only marginally so. Policy subsystems are forums where actors discuss policy issues and persuade and bargain in pursuit of their interests. During the process of their interaction with other actors, they often give up or modify their objectives in return for concessions from other members of the subsystem. These interactions, however, occur in the context of various institutional arrangements surrounding the policy process and affecting how the actors pursue their interest and ideas and the extent to which their efforts succeed (Howlett and Ramesh, 1995:51).

Actors in the policy process may be either individuals or groups. There is, however, almost an infinite variety of actors who may be members of policy subsystems and participate in the policy process, which makes the task of preparing a comprehensive catalogue virtually impossible (Howlett and Ramesh, 1995: 51-52). Howlett and Ramesh (1995:51) divided the policy actors in three broad categories i.e., organization of the society, organization of the state and organization of the international system.

Based on the above theoretical discussion, I would try to discuss the policy subsystem of Rajashahi City Corporation and highlight who are the dominant actors in the policy process. Generally, there are three types of actors involved in the policy subsystem of RCC. These are State, Society and Corporation Parishad. Now, questions can be raised who are the dominant actors? *State* does not have any direct influence on the policy making process of RCC but can exert indirect influence as the RCC depends fully on the central government grants for its development budget. Besides, it can also exert influence through the political parties and the minister[3] in charge of the city. However, in the case of RCC, the Mayor belongs to the political party which is now in power. So, government sometimes tries to get thing done[4] through the Mayor. *Society* does not have any influence in the policy making process of RCC. Generally, society in the form of civil society organization plays an important role in the development process. But in Rajshahi, the trend of emerging civil society organization is poor. There is only one civil society organization in Rajshahi which is called Nagorik Committee

(Citizen Committee). But this organization can not do any thing at all as it suffers from partisan political biasness. Most of the leaders of this organization belong to the left wing politics. Moreover, Rajshahi City Corporation is now dominated by the supporter of ruling Bangladesh Nationalist Party (BNP) and its allies. They have a strong political base in Rajshahi. On the other, the leaders of the civil society organization do not have any strong political base. They can not mobilize people. That is why, they can not influence the policy making of RCC. The whole policy process of RCC is dominated by the *Corporation Parishad* as Rajshahi City Corporation Ordinance, 1987 confers it absolute authority. According to the law, every matter related to the development of RCC has to be approved by the Corporation Parishad. The existence of the actors in the policy subsystem may be depicted by the following figure:

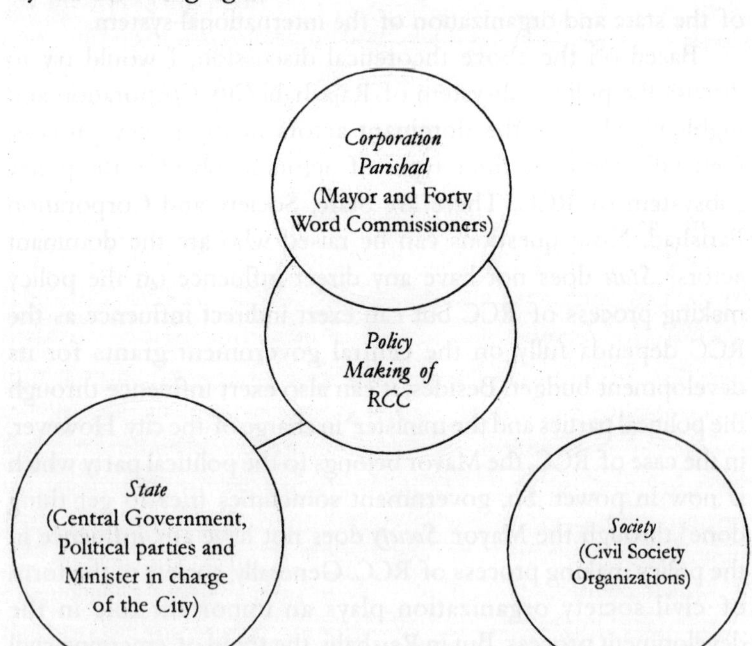

Figure[5] 2 : *Policy Subsystem of RCC*

The above figure shows the mapping of policy subsystem of RCC. It can be said that policy process is mainly dominated by the Corporation Parishad. The state through several mechanisms tries to exert an indirect influence on the policy process and becomes successful. But, the society can not influence policy process at all. Civil society organizations are in no position to persuade the policy process of RCC as they suffer from weak organizational base at Rajshahi.

PROCESS OF POLICY FORMULATION OF RCC

All the policies of RCC are passed in the Corporation Parishad that consists of Mayor, thirty elected ward commissioners and ten elected women commissioners. Actually, in RCC, there is no policy[6] as such. They take decision on various projects undertaken by various departments. During the later part of the financial year, every department makes their demands notifying various projects for the forth coming financial year. The normal process is that, each department places their demands before the concerned Standing Committee. Currently, there are eleven Standing Committees in RCC. Then, the demands of each department are considered and recommended in their respective Standing Committee meetings. After the demands are recommended, it is placed before the Corporation Parishad meeting for approval. Finally, it is passed by the majority votes of the Parishad. The total policy making process of RCC may be depicted by the following figure.

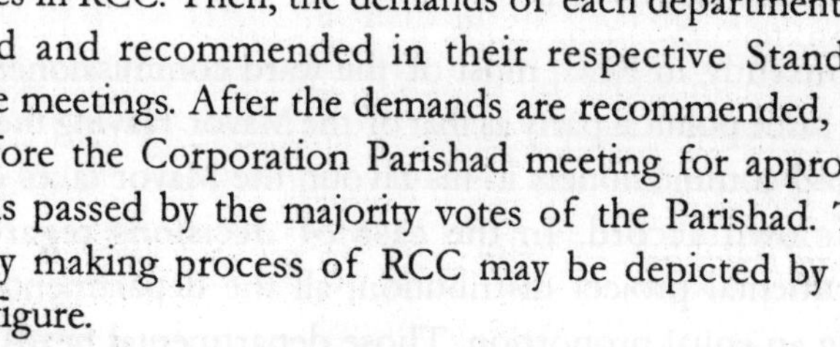

Figure 3 : *Policy Making Process of RCC*

The above discussion portrays the formal decision making process of RCC. But in practice, the whole decision making process is dominated by the Mayor. Mayor's preferences are approved in the Corporation Parishad meeting. Besides, the Standing Committees are not effective[7] in true sense. Three women members hold the view that:

> "They are not given the membership in the standing committees as equal to the general ward commissioners. If they are made members of various standing committees, their proposal and recommendations are always overruled. Actually, the Corporation Parishad is dominated by Mayor and some ward commissioners who are close to Mayor".

Another women commissioner expressed that:

> "In the last one and half year, none of her projects has been accepted by the Corporation Parishad". She continued,
>
> "We are very much neglected by the ward commissioners and the Mayor. We are like dolls. We do not have any value to them. I am really doubtful whether they consider us as commissioners or not".

Currently, in RCC, most of the ward commissioners belong to the same political party as that of the Mayor. Having the majority of word commissioners in his favour, the Mayor takes decisions on his own accord. In the case of decisions regarding the departmental project distribution, all the departments are not getting an equal proportion. Those departmental heads who are close to Mayor and have good relations with some of the influential ward commissioners are getting more projects than others. Although it is said that the decision making process of RCC is based purely on democratic principle, but in actual practice, the total decision making process is dominated by the Mayor and his associates. This type of situation is called patriminialism[8] which is characterized by rule of preference of one or several actors. It is the one man show where the Mayor is the decisive factor in every case.

IMPLEMENTATION OF INFRASTRUCTURE POLICY OF RCC

As such there is no infrastructure policy of RCC. The responsibility of infrastructural development is vested on the engineering department[9]. The engineering department approves a number of projects relating to the development of infrastructure of RCC every year. Afterward, they implement these projects. In this study 'infrastructure policy' denotes those projects that are initiated and implemented by the engineering department for the development of total infrastructure of RCC.

Following the RCC's approval of the fund regarding concerned projects, the Tender Committee determines a fixed date and other issues pertaining to implementation of the project. This Tender Committee is composed of a Chief Administrative Officer, Chief Executive Engineer, Assistant Engineer and the concerned ward commissioner. The tender schedule is prepared on the basis of market price. Tender is called through different newspapers. Many contractors participate in the tender. Each participating contractor deposits certain amount of money to the RCC office through pay-order.

Tenders are opened in front of the contractors present on a fixed date. The work is entrusted to that contractor who agrees to conduct the construction work through certain standard criteria and at competitive prices. The Engineering office, however, examines whether the tender bid of the contractor is rational. The other contractors except the winning one withdraw the money deposited by them. The contractor shoulders all responsibilities for the implementation of the project. The Figure 4 shows process involved in the implementation of the projects related to the infrastructural development.

Another important phase of the project implementation is supervision. This is done in two ways: (1) Official supervision and (2) People's supervision. The following persons are involved in the process of supervision of the implementation work of the project.

Ward Commissioner

Executive Engineer

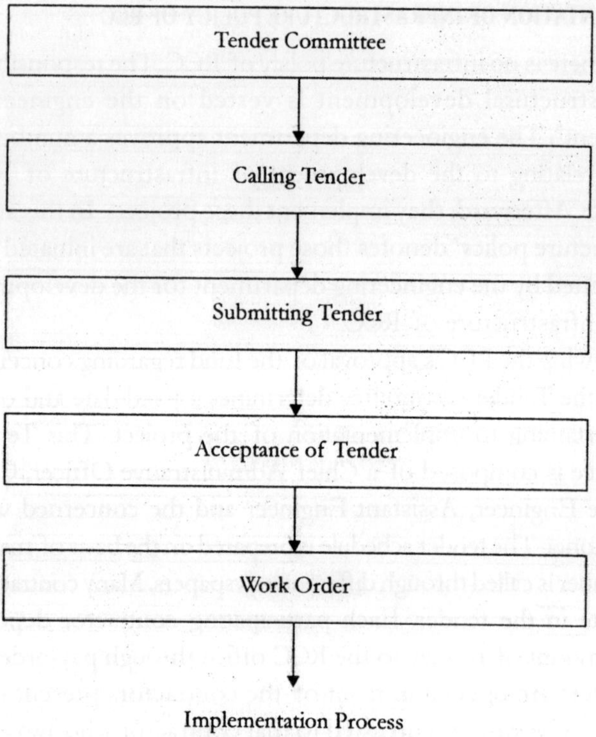

Figure 4 : *Implementation of the Infrastructure Policy of RCC*

Assistant Engineer

Sub-assistant Engineer

Work Assistant Officer

Road Inspector.

The Ward Commissioner supervises development projects under his ward with the hope of being elected as local representative in future and as part of his official duty. During the period when the work of the project goes on, the Road assistant, Work assistant and the Sub-assistant Engineer continuously supervise while the Assistant Engineer and the Executive Engineer supervise from time to time.

The contractor informs the Ward Commissioner and the Engineering office when the work of the project is complete. On receipt of the information, the Chief Executive Engineer examines whether the work has been done as per plan and they have an on-the-spot review of the standard of work. Then, they make recommendations on the work. After this, the contractors submit the bill for payment. Bills can not be raised without being certified by the ward commissioner. Since, Commissioner's certification is necessary for a final bill, he, for logical reasons, should pay attention to the standard and measurement of the work. The Commission examines the work and signs the bill. Then the contractor forwards the bills to the Engineering office. The bill is then sent to the Mayor for approval. These steps are shown in the figure below:

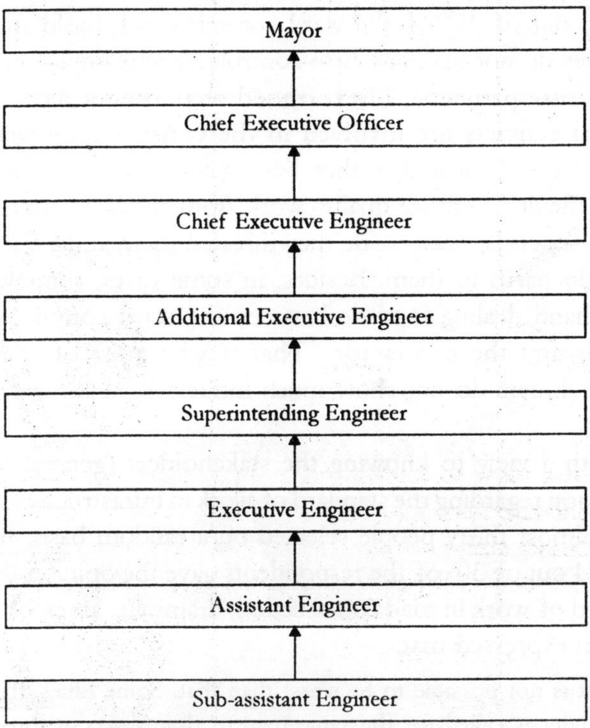

Figure 5 : *Procedure of Payment of Bills by RCC*

When the Mayor signs the bills, the file returns to the Contractor following the same steps (top-down). A cheque is then issued in favour of the contractor from the accounts office. It may be mentioned that a Contractor deposit 10% of the estimated cost of the project before he starts the project. The time-limit for maintenance is six months. If, within six months no faults are discovered in the work, he gets back the money. Otherwise, he is obliged to complete the work properly once again.

The above discussion tells the theoretical aspects of the implementation of the infrastructure of RCC. But in actual practice the scenario is different. Word commissioner's perception regarding their role in control and supervision of various ongoing projects, does not indicate any positive trend. More than 60% (6 out of 10) of the ward commissioners hold the view that, they do not have any firm control over the implementation of various projects. They argued that now-a-days, many political activists are involved in the construction sector. If they get the work and if they belong to the ruling party, it is very difficult to ensure quality work from them. If some body tries to supervise their work, they threaten them and some times could do harm to them. Besides, in some cases, some sort of under hand dealing is made between the ward commissioners, officials and the contractors. That is why most of the ward commissioners do not show much interest to supervise all the projects.

With a view to knowing the stakeholders (general public) perception regarding the standard of work in infrastructure sector, I met almost thirty people selected on a random basis. Almost 80% (24 out of 30) of the respondents gave the opinion that the standard of work in road construction, drains etc. are poor. Some of them expressed that:

> "It is not possible to be worst than that. Some times, the tender is called for the same road or drains two or three times in a year".

The respondents have identified some reasons for the decreasing quality of the infrastructure services:

(1) One of the causes is that 30%-40% of the projects are sold to the second or third party[10] (contractor) before the projects starts its journey.

(2) Some times projects are sold to the ruling party activities. In that case, no one tries to interfere in their work for fear of being harassed or in loosing the jobs.

(3) During the time of election, the contractors provide financial support to the commissioners and the mayor with the hope that they would help them in securing contracts after they were elected. As a result, elected commissioners and the mayor remains under the grip of the contractors.

(4) Due to lack of proper monitoring by the engineering department.

(5) Sometimes, a group of young people takes financial benefits from the contractors and helps them to finish their work in any way. Specially, it is done by the young political activists of the ruling party. As they posses some sort of control over the administration and political leaders, the common people fear them. No one wants to lodge protest against them.

(6) Corruption during the time of issuing license to the contractors. Quality and requirements are not examined during issuing of license.

It has been mentioned that, the quality of the construction work undertaken by RCC is below the standard. No action from the part of the RCC officials is taken to improve the quality of work. When RCC authority is doing nothing, the stakeholders (general people) should make protest against all those wrong deeds. It is the right of the common people to avail better services from the RCC. That is why the general public was asked whether they can resist the contractors from doing the work wrongly. In response to this question, 60% (18 out of 30) hold the view that they can not resist or protest against the contractors. Some of them expressed that,

> "The general people directly can not resist, but they can make complain to the Mayor and Commissioners when they come to supervise the place. But, no fruitful action is taken. Because, the contractors are more powerful as they have linkages with the Mayor, Commissioners and officials of the City Corporation. If some body tries to protest, they are identified as terrorist and are punished". Another group of people told that,

> "The Contractors first bribe some influential people in the locality and then start the work. If some body protests, they use those influential people to get rid of chaotic situations by showing fear or giving benefits".

From the above discussion it is found that, the real scenario of the construction work of RCC is not quite satisfactory. All most all the actors are involved in corruption and trying to maximize their own benefits. As a result of that, poor quality urban services are provided to the general public who do not possess any power to protest or resist them from doing so.

INVOLVED GOVERNMENT DEPARTMENTS FOR THE DEVELOPMENT OF INFRASTRUCTURE SECTOR OF RCC

In the preceding section, we discussed the formal procedure of the implementation of the various projects that are carried out for the development of the infrastructure sector within RCC. RCC can not perform all the construction work independently within its area. There are few government and autonomous departments who are sharing the ownership of the various roads and drains. So, while performing their task, they are to deal with those government offices. There are at least two government departments and one autonomous department working for the development of infrastructure of Rajshahi City along with RCC. These government departments are:

(1) Roads and Highways Department (here after, R&HD)
(2) Local Government Engineering Department (here after, LGED)
(3) Rajshahi Development Authority (here after, RDA)

Roads and Highways Department (R&HD)[11]

The Roads and Highways Department (R&HD) was created in 1962 when the old 'Construction & Building (C&B) organization was split into 2 separate bodies (the other being Public Works Department. R&HD works under the ministry of communication and is responsible for the construction and the maintenance of the major road and bridge network of Bangladesh. Since the Department was established the size of the major road network in Bangladesh has grown from 2,500 kms to the present network of just over 20,000 kms. It is responsible for an annual budget (2002/3) of approximately Taka 2,900 crore (equivalent to 496575342 US dollars), of which about Taka 2,500 Crore (equivalent to 428082191US dollars) is from the Annual Development Budget and Taka 400 crore (equivalent to 68493150 US dollars) from the Revenue Budget. The total number of posts in the Department is almost 20,000.

R&HD is responsible for national highways and important feeder roads. RCC has several feeder roads within its territory. The development and maintenance of such roads is done by the R&HD.

Local Government Engineering Department (LGED)[12]

The Local Government Engineering Department (LGED) is playing a pivotal role in rural infrastructure development. People at large in rural Bangladesh are now enjoying the benefits of LGED's different rural development projects. Rural infrastructure development projects undertaken by LGED are contributing a great deal towards the socio-economic development in the country along with the development of communication and market networks. Various activities under different projects have created short and long term employment opportunities for the poverty-stricken people. Similarly, LGED's infrastructure development activities, slum development activities and other socio-economic development activities in the urban areas have been creating employment opportunities and contributing towards environmental promotion.

To administer the Rural Works Programme (RWP) nation-wide which was started in the early 1960s, the Programme Wing (WPW) was created in 1982 under the Local Government Division (LGD) of the Ministry of Local Government, Rural Development & Co-operatives (MLGRD&C). It was converted into the Government Revenue Budget in October, 1984 as Local Govt. Engineering Bureau. LGEB was upgraded as the Local Government Engineering Department (LGED) in August, 1992. Within the RCC, various infrastructure development projects are run by LGED where they need to correspond with each other.

Rajshahi Development Authority (RDA)[13]

With a view to building a planned town in the divisional headquarters of Rajshahi, the then government established the Rajshahi Town Development Authority (RTDA) by an ordinance on October 19, 1976. Later it was renamed the Rajshahi Development Authority (RDA). This is an autonomous body and run by chairman and boards. Most members of the boards are government officials. Chairman of RDA is a deputed government official in the rank and status of additional secretary. RDA had taken up a master plan for its 177 square kilo meters area in 1978 and developed residential and commercial areas, built streets, bus terminal, big markets, parks, etc. by 1984. Then it took up the second master plan in 2000, extending its area to 322 sq. km. This plan has three phases—a five-year-long Detailed Area Plan, 10-

year-long Urban Area Plan and 20-year-long Structure Plan. The RDA has so far established four residential areas with 1,245 plots. Four other residential areas with 935 plots are under processing. It has built the 0.76 km Natore-Rajshahi-Chapainawab-ganj road[14], 1.5 km Kalpona-Sericulture[15] road and extended the Greater Road by 3.52 km. Work on construction of the 3.45 km Connecting Road from Greater Road to Bypass Road is going on and a project of another 3.3km road is awaiting approval. The RDA built three markets with 862 shops and a bus terminal. Work on the construction of a large inter-district bus terminal with the capacity of accommodating 600 buses is going on (*Source*: RDA publication). For the recreation of the city dwellers, it has built a common park and a children's park in the city and has undertaken plans to build an amusement park and a floating restaurant on the bank of the river Padma[16]. From the above discussion it is revealed that, for the development of infrastructure sector of Rajshahi City, RDA and RCC are working together. That is why, it is very important to ensure effective coordination among them.

CONCLUSION

From the above discussion it is found that theoretically, policy of RCC is formulated in the Corporation Parishad in a democratic way, but in actual practice the total process is dominated by the Mayor and his associates. The qualities of the services that are provided in the infrastructure sector by RCC are below the standard. This is because of the involvement of all parties in corruption. The general people do not have any say in this regard. Their protests are always overruled. Another important finding is that, RCC can not perform all the work independently. They are to deal with various government and autonomous departments that are also working in this sector. That is why, the question of coordination is very important in this regard.

NOTES

1. Corporation Parishad is the highest decision making body of RCC.

2. The figure is drawn by the author based on the information collected during the field study from RCC.
3. In Bangladesh, the ruling party distributes responsibility of strengthening its political base in the local level and to expedite development programme to one minister in charge of one or two district. These ministers are often called as minister in charge of the district from the partisan perspective. They bear this responsibility along with their official portfolio for the betterment of the political party whom he has nominated. If, there is no minister in one district, in that case, the minister in charge from the closets district are given responsibility of that district too.
4. If the Mayor belongs to the ruling party, central government insists him to initiate projects on the sector where government stresses emphasis. The Mayor then tries to act based on government's direction.
5. The figure is drawn by the author based on Howlett and Ramesh, (1995:51).
6. Like the central government, the RCC do no have different policies like, health policy, education policy, infrastructure policy etc. They undertake various projects for the development of different sectors. For example, for the development of the infrastructure of RCC, they undertake several projects in the beginning of each financial year. They do not call all these projects as infrastructure policy.
7. Ineffective in the sense that, Standing Committees do not run as per law. Sometimes, the Standing Committees do not even hold its monthly meeting.
8. A detailed discussion about 'patrimonialism' has been made in the second chapter. For more detail, please refer chapter two of the thesis.
9. The engineering department is one the most important department of RCC that deals with infrastructure development and construction works.
10. In Bangladesh, in every sphere of construction sector it is seen that, the contractor who gets the work order sells it to another contractor in exchange of profits. The second party sells it to the

third party. In every case, each party is selling it in exchange of some amount of profit. In that case, the last party who has already given an amount to the second party as profit tries to maximize his profit from the work. Besides, they are to give a certain portion to the engineering department and the local ward commissioner. Therefore, questions may be raised about the quality of the work.

11. All information used in this point was collected from various publications of R&HD.
12. Discussion in this point is made based of information collected from LGED office.
13. All information used in this point was collected from various publications of RDA.
14. Name of a road that covers three district of Rajshahi divisions. Three districts are Rajshahi, Natore and Chapainawab-ganj.
15. This is also a name of a road that starts from Kolpana (name of place in the Rajshahi city) to Sericulture (name of another place) Within RCC. All these are main roads.
16. Padma is a name of river that flows by the south side of Rajshahi city.

5

Intra-Organizational Coordination: Is It Necessary for Policy Implementation?

INTRODUCTION

This chapter[1] addresses the following questions: (i) do institutionalization of rules and regulations affect intra-organizational coordination? (ii) does financial management influence intra-organizational coordination? and (iii) does intra-organizational coordination affect policy implementation of urban governance in Bangladesh? As we have already stated that the main purpose of the research is to understand how intra-organization coordination affects the policy implementation of RCC, the chapter analyses to what extent service provision of RCC is well orchestrated between and among various departments?

INSTITUTIONALIZATION OF RULES AND REGULATIONS AND INTRA-ORGANIZATIONAL COORDINATION

Rules are important for the operation of any organization as these act as the guide to the workers of the organization. Rules are to some extent the formalization of logic of appropriateness. They serve as guides for newcomers to an organization, or attempts to create more uniform understandings of what those logics are (March and Olsen, 1995). These are the mechanisms which in a way guide coordinated action of the various organizations to deliver better services. Rules are institutionalized when it is infused with the values of an organization (Selznick, 1957). The workers of an organization became habituated to abide by these rules when it is established in organization's memory. So, institutionalization of rules structure activities e.g. who will do what when and how. The coordination among various departments within an organization largely depends on the extent that the rules are clearly specified and everybody is well aware of his/her responsibility.

In the case of Rajshahi City Corporation, it operates on the basis of Rajshahi City Corporation Act, 1987.This act is almost one and half decades old and there is no guideline regarding how to maintain relation and coordination among various departments. Administration runs in its own way. There is hardly any rule in RCC that may guide the officials to coordinate their activities. No department within City Corporation can act independently. For example, in the case of the implementation of infrastructure policy, the main responsibility is vested with the Engineering Department. But, the Engineering Department is heavily dependent on the Accounts Department for funds and on the Press and Publication Department for calling tender and bids. So, for the successful implementation of the infrastructure policy, it is necessary that all those departments are coordinated based on the institutional rules.

Types of Intra-organizational Relationship

Success of an organization deepens on the extent of its intra-organizational relationship. From that perspective it is important to know about the existing pattern of intra-organization relationship that exist within RCC. With a view to collecting information regarding the types of relationship that existed among the various departments, five options[2] were given to the City Corporation officials:

Table 1
Types of Intra-organizational Relationship

Options	*No of Respondents*
Hierarchic	1
Informal	1
Routine Based	2
Leadership Oriented	1
Objective oriented	1
Total	6

Question that was asked: "What types of relationship exist among various departments of RCC?"

The way the respondents replied in response to that question denotes a hazy picture. There is no unified way through which they maintain their relationship within RCC. Only two respondents (out of 6) were of the opinion that the basis of relationship is routine based. Among the remaining four respondents, one views the type of relationship as hierarchic, one as informal, one as leadership oriented and other as objective oriented.

From the above table, it is apparent that respondents clearly differ in their opinion while identifying types of intra-organizational relationship. There is no unified structured law for making communication with different departments within RCC. Under this circumstance it may be said that, officials of RCC often fall in dilemma while dealing with matters that needs intra-organizational cooperation as a result of which intra-organizational coordination may be affected.

Lack of Rules and Regulations

Another question was asked to the official of RCC about to what extent lack of rules and regulations create lack of coordination within the City Corporation? All (6 out of 6) the respondents hold the view that problems of coordination occurs due to lack of rules and regulations. The respondents have also identified some specific causes of lack of coordination.

(a) Because, rules are old[3] and ambiguous, not explained properly.

(b) As, the rules are not clearly explained, it is used in accordance with individual's own interpretation.

(c) There is no guideline regarding how to execute laws.

One City Corporation official gave an example about the use of vehicle facility[4]. He told that:

> "Generally the Mayor, Chief Executive officer, Chief Executive Engineer and the Chief Health officer are entitled to receive vehicle facilities from the City Corporation. In the law, this clause is not properly explained. Having taken the advantage of this lacking (unclear law), many officials are getting vehicle facilitates. As a result the City Corporation is bearing extra cost. Sometimes, it is observed that many officials try to misappropriate this ambiguity. In that situation, the Mayor falls in deep dilemma about whom to provide with vehicle facilities and whom to deny? He further expressed that:
>
> "Taking advantage of ambiguous law, the Mayor gives permission of using vehicles to those officials who are close to him".

This biased decisions on part of the Mayor in issuing permission for using RCC transportation and vehicles, creates some sort of dissatisfaction among the deprived officials. This dissatisfaction sometimes gives birth to personal jealousy among officials that in the long run creates problems of coordination while dealing with matters of intra-departmental affairs. Another City Corporation official expressed:

> "If the laws regarding the use of vehicle would be clear, that would not leave any scope for misunderstanding and personal jealously among officials which would ensure good working relationship". He further expressed that,
>
> "Successful intra-organizational coordination depends on the extent that rules and regulations are institutionalized.

> But, in the case of RCC, institutionalization of rules and regulations are totally absent".

The respondents were asked whether they feel any problem of coordination while discharging their duties and responsibilities. Almost all respondents (6 of 6) were of the opinion that they face serious problems of coordination. Further, respondents were also asked about how coordination is ensured among various departments in implementing policies? In response to this question, most of the respondents hold the view that there are no written rules and regulations for ensuring coordination. Some of the respondents expressed that coordination is ensured through coordination committee.[5] Another respondent expressed that coordination among different departments is ensured through CEO and by departmental heads at the departmental level. But every respondent stressed that there is no structured rules and regulation in RCC by which it can easily be possible to establish sound intra-organizational coordination that has a long lasting impact on the implementation of policies. So the hypothesis *'the more structured the institutional rules and regulations in terms of who will do what and when, the less will be the coordination problems in policy implementation'* may said to be supported by the findings.

FINANCIAL MANAGEMENT AND INTRA-ORGANIZATIONAL COORDINATION

Resource is an important factor for the implementation of any policy. Within the City Corporation, funds are limited but demands are unlimited. Moreover, the internal resource of RCC is inadequate. So, they have to depend fully on the government grants for the development projects. The Table 2 represents the extent of dependence of RCC on government grants:

The table reveals that more than 80% of the expenditure of RCC in last three consecutive years has been financed by the central government grants. No remarkable change has been noticed over the years regarding decrease of dependency on central government grants by raising the internal resources. Although it has been

Table[6] 2
Income and Expenditure of RCC (In Millions of USD)

Year	*Total Income (Internal Income and government grants)*		*Total Expenditure*	*% of expenditure financed by government grants*
2001-2002	*Internal income:*	3675667		
	Taxes			
	Rates			
	Fees			
	Miscellaneous etc.			
	Government grants	17245942	20921609	82%
	Development Assistant Grants 366266999			
	Project grants (ADP[7]) 640896029			
	Total Income	20921609		
2002-2003	*Internal income*	4414551		
	Taxes			
	Rates			
	Fees			
	Miscellaneous etc.			
	Government grants	20429247		
	Development Assistant Grants 432654660			
	Project grants (ADP) 760413350			
	Total Income	24843798	24843798	82%
2003-2004	*Internal income*	4950375		
	Taxes			
	Rates			
	Fees			
	Miscellaneous etc.			
	Government grants	20858979		
	Development Assistant Grants 342035608			
	Project grants (ADP) 876128777			
	Total Income	25809354	25809354	81%

observed a steady increase in the internal income but at the same time total expenditure has also increased. In spite of receiving such a large amount of government grants every year, the RCC authorities pointed out that government grants always remain lower than the demands placed by them. The problems of coordination arises when comes the question of distributing inadequate resources among various projects undertaken by various departments within RCC. Every department within the City Corporation tries to receive more resources for financing their projects. Sometimes resource distribution becomes stagnant as the authority fails to establish sound coordination among contesting demands and departments. Due to lack of sound intra-organizational coordination, some project remains half done.

While talking with the RCC officials regarding resource constraints, it is found that RCC is suffering from severe resource constraints. All respondents (6 out of 6) hold the view that there are serious resource constraints in RCC which in turn affect policy implementation. One high ranking official of RCC told that:

> "The grants which are given by the government always remain lower than the estimated budget. So, it becomes problematic for them to distribute inadequate funds among various departments". He also expressed that:
>
> "Sometimes allocation of government resources depends on the strength of relationship of mayor with the central government. But, it is not likely that every time the Mayor is successful to bring large amount of grants from the central government".

The respondents identified several reasons for the resource constraints:

(a) Too much dependency on the government grants.

(b) Government does not provide available grants according to the needs of the locality.

(c) Inadequate local resources. The government always stresses emphasis to increase internal resources but, in the case of RCC, it is a difficult task to increase local resources as Rajshahi is not an industrial city. Moreover,

> the rate of urbanization is not very high here. The only sources of income are the taxes and tolls within the City Corporation.

All these above factors create resource constraints within the City Corporation that have direct impact on the distribution of resources among various departments. The respondents were also asked whether unequal[8] resource distribution affects intra-organizational coordination or not? All respondents (6 out of 6) expressed that unequal resource management seriously affects intra-organizational coordination. Another higher official of RCC expressed his view in the following way:

> "I am not satisfied with the allocated grants for my department. Because, it is not adequate in terms of demands of my department. Moreover, government grants are not equally distributed within all the departments. Some departmental heads that have good relations with the top are getting more amount, other departments are getting less. As a result, I have to face many problems". He further added that:
>
> "Distribution of funds is not done following any clear rule. It is done arbitrarily. This is often creating dissatisfaction among different departmental heads that affect sound working relations".

From the above discussion, it may be derived that resource management is a crucial factor that affects intra-organizational coordination. It is found from the respondent's opinion that, RCC always running short of adequate financial resources. On the one hand, they do not have adequate internal resources, on the other hand, government grants always remain lower than the proposed demand. All these factors create problems of intra-organizational coordination as a result of which many project remain incomplete during implementation stages. So, our hypothesis *'the more the scarcity of financial resources, the more will be the problems of coordination'* may said to be supported by the findings.

Institutionalization of rules and norms and management of resources are not the only causes of lack of intra-organizational coordination, but also, there are some other variables too such as abuse of power that also affect the intra-organizational coordination.

ABUSE OF POWER

When power is exercised for unlawful gain or to render unlawful favour or beyond the jurisdiction of the power holder then it may be called abuse of power. In the case of RCC, as the Mayor is the executive and political head, very often he abuses power ignoring the rules and regulations that often frustrates the officials of the City Corporation. As a result, many officials are apathetic to cooperate fully and this attitude creates problems of coordination that hampers policy implementation in the long run.

The respondents were asked whether there are abuses of power within RCC. Three (out of 6) respondents expressed their opinion affirmatively and said that there are wide abuses power in RCC. One (out of 6) respondent responded negatively. And the remaining 2 expressed their opinion in between. One official of the RCC said:

> "Power is used in inappropriate manner in every level. It is not possible to control. Nobody protest against it because of fear of loosing job".

Based on the above discussion, it can be said that power is widely abused in the City Corporation that creates dissatisfaction among the officials which in the long run affect intra-organizational coordination.

INTRA-ORGANIZATIONAL COORDINATION AND POLICY IMPLEMENTATION

As various departments are involved in the implementation of infrastructure policy of RCC, it is necessary that they have a good working environment and linked by a sound coordination system with one another. While talking to the City Corporation officials, the researcher tried to know whether they think intra-organizational coordination is necessary for successful coordination and how it affects the implementation process.

At first, the respondents were asked to identify the causes of lack of intra-coordination other than lack of institutionalized rules and regulations and financial management. They identified a number of factors. These are:

(a) *Poor quality of staff:* This is because of political appointment without maintaining proper selection criteria. When some one gets appointment on the basis of political consideration, he/she tries to keep them busy in dealing with political matters rather than discharging his/her official duties. His/her nonexistence in discharging duties put additional pressure on others in order keep official momentum going. This situation creates aggravation among those who bears additional responsibilities that in the long run affects intra-organizational coordination.

(b) *Political influence on the officials:* The ruling political party leaders always try to exert influence in various issues. When a powerful political leader of the ruling party tries to gets thing done, and at the same time if the Mayor by virtue of his belongingness to opposition tries to resist, the official in charge fall in great dilemma about what to do? In that case, the dealing official tries to hide the matter as long as he could. As a result, the work gets delayed.

(c) *Due to lack of delegation of power:* Every decision within City Corporation needs to be approved by the Mayor. The Mayor himself is a busy person. Very often, he stays away from RCC. He does not delegate his power. If any urgent issue is needed to be approved by the Mayor and if Mayor stays out of station, it becomes problematic how to coordinate those things. As a result the whole process becomes stagnant and delayed.

(d) *When various departments undertake similar policy issues* problems of coordination occur regarding whose projects would be approved. In that case, the departmental heads start to pursue the matter to the Mayor and influential ward commissioners. Consequentially, projects of those departments are approved whose strength of persuasion is stronger than others. This type of decisions based on strategies gives birth to frustration among the deprived party. Those who are affected may find it difficult to maintain their loyalty and are reluctant to cooperate.

Further, the respondents were also asked do they think lack of intra-organizational coordination affects policy implementation. All the respondents (6 out of 6) hold the view that lack of intra-organizational coordination affects policy implementation. The following example may illustrate that how City Corporation suffers from serious intra-organizational coordination.

Case Reference

At one time, the RCC was evicting all illegal constructions in the City, but at the same time, the City Corporation was doing another construction work on the City Protection dam[9] in Futkipara[10] which was illegal. Nobody knew for what purpose this building was constructed. However, it was found that the construction work was going on the basis of Mayor's oral permission. One ward commissioner who was also the chairman of city development and planning committee, mentioned with a high note of discontent that he knew nothing about it.

On 10th December, 2002, the City Mayor told in a press conference that all the illegal construction within the RCC would be evicted by 17th December, 2002. This statement was totally contradictory. On the one hand, he was telling that all the illegal construction would be evacuated and on the other hand, he was giving oral permission for constructing new buildings.

> The newspaper also brought out news that the construction work was built on a dam. This might cause damage to the dam and the dam might fall apart any time and the whole city might go under water. (Sonali Sangbad[11]: 20-12-2002).

The above case may said to be an example of lack of intra-organization coordination within RCC. A construction work was going on in such a place which protects the city from flood water. From the legal point of view, this type of construction was illegal. But nobody knew why it was constructed. Even the person, who was the chairman of the city development and planning committees, did not know.

Finally the respondents were asked about the direct impact of intra-organizational coordination on the policy implementation of RCC. The respondents answered that lack of intra-organizational coordination do have negative impacts on policy implementation. As a result, policy implementation is delayed, cost is increased and unsatisfactory public services are delivered. The following table presents the answers of respondents:

Table 3
Impact of Lack of Intra-organizational Coordination on Policy Implementation (Absolute Frequency)

Options	*Delay in Project Completion (Time)*	*Cost Increase (Money)*	*Unsatisfactory Public Service delivery*
Yes	5	5	4
No	1	1	2
Respondents	6	6	6

Question that was asked: "Do you think as a result of lack of intra-organizational coordination policy implementation is delayed, cost increased and unsatisfactory public service is delivered?"

From the table it is clear that most of the respondents mentioned that lack of intra-organizational coordination causes delay in project completion, increase in the cost of projects and the services that are delivered are quite unsatisfactory. The following example shows how City Corporation is incurring excess expenditure because of lack of coordination within RCC.

Case Reference

> In a special audit report of the RCC, it is published that, very often they paid excess payment to the contractors than the actual price of the work schedule. In the financial year 1997-99, the City Corporation authority paid 9, 13,738 BDT [12](equivalent to 15,650 US dollar) as non-tender item to the contractor. On the other hand, it paid 1, 53,791 BDT (equivalent to 2650 US dollar) in access than the scheduled price.
>
> The news paper sources said that, in response of this allegation, City Corporation authority pointed out that, this was done to those projects which were not completed in due time. They also said that, it was not the fault of the contractors for delaying in project completion, but it was because of the procedural[13] delays in sanctioning the work. As the market price increased, they were paid excess amount than what was estimated in order to compensate for the rise of market price. (Sonali Sangbad[14]: 20-10-2002).

Cost increase takes place when there are delays in decision making process and delay in decision making occurs when it comes the question of maintaining various steps. After the decision is taken to allocate the project to a contractor, the file is sent by the Engineering Department for the approval to the Mayor via Accounts Department and General Administration Department. If various decision making stages are completed in due time then procedural delay may be prevented. Due to procedural delay in issuing the work order, the contractors do not complete the work in due time. As a result, cost of project implementation increases which puts extra burden on the city corporation.

CONCLUSION

In this chapter an attempt was made to analyze (i) does institutionalization of rules and regulations affect intra-organizational coordination? (ii) does financial management influence intra-organizational coordination? and (iii) does intra-organizational coordination affect policy implementation of urban governance in Bangladesh? We have found that there is a lack of institutionalization of rules and regulations as regards coordination of activities of various departments within RCC. Financial management is also important for intra-organizational coordination. RCC suffers from an inadequate financial base as well as proper allocation of resources. Lastly, it was found that lack of intra-organizational coordination seriously affects policy implementation of RCC. As a result of this, projects implementation is delayed, cost are increased and general public are deprived from getting proper urban service.

NOTES

1. Analysis of this chapter is based on information collected during interview with six City Corporation officials that includes Mayor, Chief Executive Office, Chief Executive Engineer, Chief Medical Officer, Budget Cum Accounts Officer and Public Relations Officer.

2. Five options that were given to respondents were hierarchic, informal, routine based, leadership oriented and objectives. Hierarchic denotes that the basis of relationship is based on the principle of chain of command which is seen in bureaucratic organization. Informal denotes no formal way of making communication. If problem persist, that may be solved over telephonic conversation or by meeting with the aggrieved party physically. Routine based means, corresponded are made only when it is needed. There is hardly any scope for informal communication among various departments. Leadership oriented means communication is based on the leadership quality of the departmental heads and finally objective oriented means relationship is maintained only to meet demands. This question was asked with a view to mapping the fact that whether RCC follows any unified rules regarding intra-organizational relationship or not.

3. Old in the sense that when the City Corporation Ordinance was passed in 1987, the population size of Rajshahi city was small and

the activities of the City Corporation were confined to a manageable size. As time passes, people's demands are mounting. Consequently, the activities of the City Corporation are also expanding to a wide range. That is why, very often, it becomes problematic to handle situations as every thing is not well defined in the existing law.

4. Here vehicle facility means use of transport of RCC and avail the fuel subsidy that is provided by RCC.
5. But in actual practice, there is no coordination committee in RCC for ensuring intra-organizational coordination. In 1996, the AL government established a coordination committee for every City Corporation in order to ensure inter-organizational coordination. But, Bangladesh Nationalist party (BNP) after coming into power in 2001, by an official order, discontinued the functioning of this committee.
6. The table is made by the author based on information collected from RCC and all accounts have been calculated in terms of millions of U.S. dollar (USD).
7. ADP stands for Annual Development Programme.
8. We have already discussed that RCC suffers from serious resource constraints. At the same time, it also suffers from clear and specified laws. As a result, these scarce resources are distributed among contesting departments based on the strength of relationship of the departmental heads with the Mayor ignoring the importance and priority of projects. Those departments receive much allocation whose heads are very close to the Mayor. That is why; I have used the term unequal resource distribution.
9. There is dam on the bank of the river Padma to protect the city from the flood water.
10. Futkipara is a name of place of Rajshahi City.
11. 'Sonali Sangbad' is the widely circulated local daily news paper published from Rajshahi.
12. BDT stands for Bangladeshi taka.
13. Before the work order being handed over to the contractor, the file needs approval of the Mayor number of times traveling through engineering, general administration and finance department which

is a lengthy process. The total journey is called procedure and delay in this procedure is called procedural delays. A more detailed discussion about the procedure has been discuses in the fourth chapter.

14. 'Sonali Sangbad' is a widely circulated local daily news paper published from Rajshahi.

6

INTER-ORGANIZATIONAL COORDINATION: DOES IT MATTER FOR POLICY IMPLEMENTATION?

INTRODUCTION

The objective of this chapter[1] is two-fold, *first* to delineate how central-local relationship affects inter-organizational coordination and *second* to understand how democratic vs. bureaucratic accountably influences inter-organizational coordination during policy implementation of urban governance in Bangladesh.

CENTRAL-LOCAL RELATIONS AND INTER-ORGANIZATION COORDINATION

The question of autonomy is an important variable in the study of central-local relations. Although the urban-local government bodies in Bangladesh enjoy a degree of operational autonomy they are in no way independent of the central government of the overall administrative system of the country. As a result, there are a number of areas of interaction between an urban body and the government, which cover legal, operational and financial matters as well as control and supervision by the government. Here, our main concern is to analyze the types of central-local relations[2] that exist in urban governance in Bangladesh and how these relations affect inter-agency coordination which has a long lasting impact on the implementation of policies.

Types of Relationship

In order to map the impact of central-local relationship on inter-organizational coordination, a question was asked to the respondents from the Rajshahi City Corporation (here after RCC) regarding the type of relationship that existed among the City Corporation and central government specially with regard to the Ministry of Local Government, Rural development and Cooperatives (LGRD and Cooperatives)[3].

Almost all the respondents (6 out of 7) replied affirmatively mentioning the existence of positive relationship between RCC and central government. Further, the respondents mentioned that the positive relationship is because of the Mayor's[4] political affiliation with (BNP)[5] which is now the party in power. Moreover, the Mayor has a powerful position in the party. Along with the position of Mayor ship, he is also the Member of the Parliament (MP) of Bangladesh and one of the organizing secretaries of the party. These factors were crucial for a positive relationship with the central government. At the same time, the respondents also mentioned central-local relationship varies depending on the nature[6] of the central government. They expressed that during 1996-2001, the scenario was different since the government was run by Awami League (AL) which is now the party in opposition. The RCC had to suffer lot of problems specially, in the allocation of resources as the Mayor belonged to the opposition BNP. The tendency of the central government is to provide more advantages to those City Corporations that are dominated by their party men.

Central-local relationship is also manifested by the form of fund mobilization and conflict between autonomy versus centralization. These two variables affect central-local relationship directly.

Problems in Fund Mobilization

The success of any development projects largely depends on the availability of its funds. In the case of RCC, most of the development projects are financed by the government grants. So mobilization of funds from the central government depends on the type of relationship that City Mayor establishes with central government. In order to highlight this issue, a question was asked to the respondents about problems of funds mobilization. All the respondents (6 out of 6) expressed that there are serious difficulties in mobilizing funds. This is because,

(a) Most of the development programmes of the city corporation are financed by central government grants. The normal procedure is that City Corporation places their demands in the form of budget for the ensuing financial year to the government and the government accordingly decides the amount of grant. In most of the cases, there remain a huge gap between proposed demands and approved grants. In such a situation, Mayor's political image is a crucial factor. Government approves more grants to a city corporation that has the capacity to make successful lobbying. In this case, Mayor's political image and party affiliation are crucial factors.

(b) At times, even the approved funds are not released in due time. This happens mostly when the Mayor belongs to the opposition party. This is causing serious problems in the implementation of various projects that keeps many projects half-done or under completion. The following example would substantiate the argument.

Case Reference

Rajshahi city has for long been faced with crisis of drinking water, especially in the dry season. The City Corporation authorities said extraction capacity of its pumps declined by about 25 per cent in summer. With a view to provide city

> dwellers with safe drinking water, the Rajshahi City Corporation opened the first of the three water treatment plants in September, 2003. According to the Department of Public Health Engineering, works on the other two were going on in full swing and were scheduled to be completed by December, 2003. The Rajshahi City Corporation water supply department said it would provide city residents with only 45 million litres of water a day against the demand for some 103 million litres.
>
> Rajshahi City Mayor said that the construction of these projects would have been completed five years back if they would have received full cooperation from the then AL government. The Mayor mentioned that the initiative to install water treatment plans to address excessive hardness of water was taken up in 1994. The ministry concerned approved of the project in early 1995 and the Executive Committee of the National Economic Council approved of a Tk 56-crore (equivalent to 9589041 US dollars) project on December 19, 1995. The public health engineering department was entrusted with the project implementation.
>
> Work on the first phase of the project started on April 1, 1996, scheduled for a June 1998 completion. But it could not be implemented as per schedule because of cold shoulder shown by the then Awami League government. The project was left half way for fund constraints. The money was released after the four-party alliance government led by BNP comes to power and the work resumed and completed. (Holiday, Internet Edition, Country News, 26 September, 2003).

The above example denotes that the central-local relations are a determining factor for inter-organizational relationship. Lack of coordination has affected the implementation of water plant projects of RCC seriously. As a result, common peoples are victimized. If the RCC authority would have received full cooperation from the central government in releasing funds, the projects would have been completed five years back and the general public would have been enjoyed the benefits till then.

Autonomy versus Centralization

RCC is administered by the Rajshahi City Corporation Ordinance, 1987. But, in regards to its autonomy, the law itself is ambiguous. On the one hand, the law talks about local autonomy of the RCC and on the other hand, it provides central government enormous powers to exercise control over RCC. Some of the more important issues can be enumerated below through which central government exercise control (Siddique, 2000:156-157):

(a) the central government makes laws and rules there under for all local bodies, including the RCC; and it can also control the RCC through the so-called standing orders;

(b) the Mayor may be removed from office at any time, without assigning any reason; the government may also supersede the entire RCC or suspend a Department of the RCC;

(c) the government may assign any function to the RCC; similarly, it can also take away any function from the RCC at any time;

(d) the RCC budget must be approved by the central government;

(e) the government may call for any records of the RCC;

(f) the government can inspect the RCC at any time;

(g) the RCC has to send the central government an annual report on its activities;

(h) for forming additional standing committees, the RCC must obtain the permission of the government;

(i) the schedule of posts in the RCC has to be sanctioned by the government, and no appointment beyond the schedule is allowed;

(j) the RCC can not directly negotiate with foreign donors or private investors; and

(k) the Chief Executive Officer (CEO) is appointed by the government, and he has considerable powers; he is the custodian of all records; he is allowed to take measures during an emergency; he is allowed to be present in all Corporation/standing committee meetings; he can hardly be censured by the RCC, and he is the appointing authority for all subordinate posts.

As we have already mentioned those issues through which central government exercise its control over RCC, it is imperative to make some comments in this respect. If central government makes laws for the City Corporation, there should not be any problem, but the worrying fact is that they (central government) do not allow the City Corporation to deliver their inputs in the law making process[7]. The City Corporation is always either by passed or over ruled. Besides, the existing provisions for removal of the Mayor, supercession of the Corporation and suspension of particular Departments of the RCC by the central government clearly shows sign of highhandedness and authoritarianism which goes against the spirit of the Constitutional provision on local government. Another issue that should be mentioned here that, these mechanisms are used viciously when the party in power in the central government is opposed to the Mayor's political party. Another mechanism that central government uses to control the City Corporation is the deputation of CEO in the City Corporation having power, prestige and status next to the Mayor. So, there are several areas and issues of conflicts between autonomy of urban bodies vs. control of central government.

With a view to mapping the impact of these conflicts and how they affect lack of coordination, the respondents were asked to discuss their views regarding the nature of the contrast between autonomy and centralization in RCC. All most all the respondents hold the view that there is a serious conflict in RCC. The problem is associated with the deputation of CEO in the RCC who belongs to the Bangladesh Civil Service (BCS). Being a government official he perceives himself as superior to other City Corporation officials which at times creates frustration among the officials. This usually leaves negative impact on the working environment. One official expressed his opinion in the following way:

> "As the CEO is deputed by the central government, he suffers from a superiority complexity. He does not bother the RCC officials. Besides, the Mayor is a very busy person who can not stay in Corporation all the time. The absence of Mayor has made him more powerful". He further stated:
>
> "This type of conflict creates problematic working environment that hampers the overall development process".

From the foregoing discussion it is found that, central-local relationship is important for the successful coordination in the implementation of any policy. This relationship is imperative especially in the case of funds mobilization from the central government. The problem takes a serious shape if the Mayor belongs to the opposition party. But in the case of Rajshahi City Corporation, it is evident that, currently there exists a sound working relationship with the central government. This is because of the political image of the Mayor. But it is also true that, in spite of having a very positive relationship with the central government, there are problems with regard to the fund management which sometimes create coordination problems in the whole development process. As a result of this, the total policy implementation is jeopardized. So the hypothesis *'the more the access to central-government, the lesser will be the problems of coordination in policy implementation'* may said to be supported to some extent by the findings. The situation is worse when the Mayor is having the opposite political color. The situation may be better if the party in power and Mayor have the same color. However, finance/fund is always a problem irrespective of Mayor's political color. But the situation could be worse if there is a mismatch of political color. This is the situation prevailing in RCC.

DEMOCRATIC VERSUS BUREAUCRATIC ACCOUNTABILITY AND ITS INFLUENCE ON INTER-ORGANIZATIONAL COORDINATION

There is a sharp distinction between the City Corporation and various government departments with regard to their mode of operation and accountability patterns. City Corporations are political organs and popularly elected and possess an autonomous status. Therefore, political leadership is responsible to common citizen for every action. On the other hand, government departments are staffed by civil servants who are accountable to their line ministries in a hierarchic manner. Besides, due to colonial legacy, the bureaucrats hold a pre-eminent position in the political system of the Bangladesh. Taking advantage of the political squabbles and the incompetence and inexperience of politicians, the bureaucrats usurp political power (Zafarullah *et. al,* 1997). Bureaucrats differ from politicians in terms of education and social status also. Bureaucrats are highly educated than that of politicians and hold a prestigious position in the society. More over, bureaucrats mostly reside in the urban area where as politicians reside in the periphery.

As we have already mentioned, in the implementation of infrastructure policy of the RCC, it deals with various government offices that are working parallel with the city corporation. With a view to mapping the issue of inter-organizational coordination problems and its influence on the policy implementation of the RCC, several questions were asked to the government officials.

Problems of Coordination

A question that was asked to the government officials whether they perceive any problem of coordination while working with the city corporation. The respondents answered the question in the following way. The majority of the respondents (4 out of 7) hold the view that they felt problems of coordination while working with the city corporation. But the rest expressed the opposite view. One government official expressed:

> "There are some roads within the city corporation whose ownership belongs to Roads and Highways Department (R&HD). But, the maintenance and development works are done by the city corporation. The normal procedure is that before initiating the process of maintenance or development works, the city corporation needs prior permission from the Roads and Highways Department. If the City Corporation authority applies for permission, after feasibility analysis, they issue permission on the behalf of the department. But in actual practice, the city corporation authority does not bother about having prior permission before commencing on any development work and they do not even inform the departments when they would do what."
> He further stated:
> "When we come to know of this type of initiative, we try to prevent them form doing so. In that situation, the development works remain half finished as the RCC authorities do not communicate properly and in due time".

The above statements denote that there exist problems associated with cooperation between these two organizations that affect policy implementation. If a project remains half way for months, the common people suffer. In the following paragraph we would discuss a case that might illustrate that there are serious problems of coordination between RCC and various government departments.

Case Reference[8]

> The Roads and Highways Department, Rajshahi made a 'Jatri Sauni'[9] by the road side of center of Laxmipur[10] in 2001.The ownership and maintenance of this building belonged to the Roads and Highways Department. But, all of a sudden, the RCC, violating all the rules and regulations and norms, divided that 'Jatri Saouni' into two by a dividing

wall in 2003. Later on, they gave it as lease to some individuals. Now it has been changed into shops. Some informal sources said that, some officials of the RCC did this unlawful act by accepting bribe of some 8 millions BDT[11] (15000 us dollars).

The Roads and Highways Department after being informed started formal correspondence with RCC authorities requesting them for breaking the divider and evacuating the shop keepers from that position. Altogether, R&HD authority sent four letters to the RCC authority. But, unfortunately, no action had been taken by the RCC authority. The R&HD did not even receive any letter from the RCC regretting for that action. As a result of this non cooperation from the RCC, the ultimate suffers are the common people who are deprived from using that 'Jatri Sauni'. This example showed that there remains a serious problem of coordination between city corporation and different government offices. Another high ranking government official stated:

"The RCC authority because of having more power and local influence than that of the government agencies ignore government officials and deem themselves superior. For instance, the Chief Executive Engineer of RCC has the same rank and status like him (Executive Engineer of R&HD Department), but the way he acts reflect his superiority complex and lead to discontentment among the government officials. This sense of false pride creates differences that fosters lack of coordination and ultimately hampers policy implementation."

The discussion above reflects the reality that problems arise more because of arrogance of RCC in relation to central bureaucracy and the bureaucracy feels that they are overdriven by RCC in policy implementation. These types of realization on the part of the government officials impede a positive working relationship with the RCC. As a result,policy implementation suffers.

Influence of Mayor

Abusing formal positions while in power in order to grant undue favour and benefit to one's relatives, friends and key supporters is a hall-mark of politics in Bangladesh (Khan: *http://www.ti-bangladesh.org/docs/research/MKhan.htm*). The case of urban governance in Bangladesh in this regard is no exception. As the Mayor is a political personality, he uses this position to influence government officials for getting something done in his own favour. With a view to achieve a clear understanding about this issue, a question was asked to the government officials whether they felt any pressure while discharging their duties and responsibilities. They replied in the following way.

Table 1
Influence of Mayor on Government Officials

Options	*No. of Respondents*
Yes	4
No	3
Total	7

Question that was asked: "Do government officials feel any pressure from the Mayor while discharging their duties"?

The majority of the respondents (4 out of 7) were of the opinion that they felt pressure while discharging their duties and responsibilities. One government official expressed his views in the following way.

> "Sometimes, the mayor tries to influence some cases over telephone. When we talk about the rules and regulations, he insisted us to do our best. As he is a respectable and most powerful person, we can not deny his request." He further viewed:
>
> "This is a dilemma for us, especially when the Mayor belongs to the political party in power. We do not want to make him annoyed. After all, we have to secure our job".

Another government official expressed his opinion in the following way:

> "As a people representative, he is more powerful than me. Besides, he has the power to influence government planning. That is why: very often, he tries to influence various government departments".

From the above statements, it is obvious that there is a strong pressure from the Mayor on the government officials. In most cases, they could not do otherwise for fear of being transferred or loosing jobs. But problems in the form of harassment start when they deny entertaining undue influence.

Control on the Implementation of Policies of RCC

Where there is a question of sharing the responsibility between the government offices and RCC with regard to the policy implementation, there must be the scope for evaluation, monitoring and control of activities by both parties. If one party dominates the process of implementation and the other party is neglected in every case, the existence of sound working relationship becomes a problem. In order to know the control mechanism and evaluation criteria of those projects of RCC where various government departments are involved, the officials were asked whether they have any control on implementation of those projects of RCC.

Table 2
Control by Government
Officials on the Implementation of Policies of RCC

Options	*No. of Respondents*
Yes	2
Little	2
No	3
Total	7

Question that was asked:"To what extent your department can impose control on the implementation of infrastructure policy of RCC?"

Majority of the respondent hold the view they do not have any control over the activities of the RCC. They can exert some sort of control where City Corporation needs prior permission from government offices to initiate development projects. In those cases, the government offices after having completed feasibility analysis, issue permission. But later on, once the development activities gets started, they do not have any control which is not the sign of sound working relationship. In the reply to the question, one government official strongly expressed that:

> "RCC authorities do not care about other government offices. They (RCC) deem themselves more powerful. Now-a-days, they are more aggressive as their Mayor is more powerful. As a result, sound coordination is not possible".

The above statement reflects that RCC authority does not even allow the government offices to monitor their activities. Whenever, government offices get the opportunity to take the upper hand, they take revenge by delaying the process of correspondence. As a result, project implementation gets delayed.

Types of Inter-organizational Relationship

A sound working relationships is important for successful policy implementation. In that case, City Corporation should have a sound and good relations with those government offices situated in Rajshahi who are involved in the processof implementation of the infrastructure policy of RCC. In order to have clear perception about this relationship, a question regarding types of relationship that exists between the city corporation and various central-government agencies was asked to the government officials. Three options were given to them. They replied in the following way:

Table 3
Types of Inter-organizational Relationship

Options	*No. of Respondents*
Sound working relationship	2
Moderate working relationship	4
Dysfunctional working relationship	1
Total	07

Question that was asked: "What types of relationships existed between government offices and City Corporation?" Three options were given to the respondents. Sound working relationship to denote positive relationship, dysfunctional working relationship to denote negative relationship and moderate working relationship to denote in between positive and negative relationship.

The majority of the respondents (4 out of 7) expressed that they have a moderate working relationship with City Corporation. Moderate relationship may not reflect the picture of having full coordination among government officials and RCC authority. In these circumstances, policy implementation may be affected. The government officials were also asked whether these relationships affect the policy implementation or not? In reply to this question, they expressed their opinion in the following way:

Table 4
Impact of Inter-organizational Relationship on Policy Implementation

Options	*No. of Respondents*
Yes	4
No	3
Total	7

Question that was asked: "Do you think type of relationship that exists between government offices and RCC affect policy implementation? Two options were given: Yes or No? If yes, how it affects?"

Majority of the respondents (4 out of 7) hold the view that these relationships affect the policy implementation and the rest (3 out of 7) expressed the opposite view. The relationship specially affect in the release of funds. Unavailability of funds does not ensure timely completion of project implementation. Some of the respondents expressed that if positive relationship existed between the government agencies and City Corporation, government grants would be available and there would be fewer problems in the release of funds. As a result, development would be expedited.

CONTRAST BETWEEN DEMOCRATIC AND BUREAUCRATIC ACCOUNTABILITY

Finally, the respondents both from City Corporation and government offices were asked is the contrast between democratic and bureaucratic accountability affect coordination among various government departments and RCC. Contrast denotes the different mode of operations and accountability patters of both the organizations. They were given two options. They replied in the following way:

Table 5
Impact of Contrast of Accountability on Policy Implementation

Options	*City Corporation Officials*	*Government Officials*
Yes	5	5
No	1	2
Respondents	6	7

Question that was asked: "It is well known that the patterns of accountability of the government officials is bottom-up and the patterns of accountability of the City Corporation is top-down. So, there is a contrast between the democratic (top-down) and bureaucratic (bottom-up) governance". Does this governance system affect the coordination among the government departments and City Corporation in regards to policy implementation? Please specify: Yes or No? If yes, why and how?"

The table reflects that in both cases, most of the respondents (5 out of 6 City Corporation officials and 5 out of 7 government officials) hold the same view that this contrast creates coordination problems and that hampers policy implementation to a large extent. They have identified some factors that are responsible for creating problems of coordination among these departments:

First, Decision making in a bureaucratic organization is a lengthy (hierarchical) process. On the other hand, decision making in RCC is very prompt if the Mayor wishes a decision to be taken quickly. That is why, the city corporation authorities expect the same speed with regard to the decision making from the government officials. But, field level bureaucrats can not do every thing in accordance with the expectation of City Corporation officials as they need approval from their line ministries in matters regarding policy issues. Different work place in these two types of organization makes policy implementation delayed.

Second, According to bureaucrats, politicians are not as transparent as they should be. They always try to capitalize their own benefits ignoring the welfare of the common people. On the other hand, the bureaucrats are not in a position to exercise power like the politicians. They (bureaucrats) argued that some times politicians create pressure on them to perform such things which is illegal. In such a situation, problems of coordination happen if they deny doing so[12].

Lastly, According to RCC officials, the bureaucrats deem themselves superior as they belong to central government service. They do not show willingness to communicate with City Corporation properly. This perception some times creates problems of coordination in dealing with each other.

From the above discussion it is found that there are problems of coordination between officials of RCC and various government departments while dealing with each other. We can refer the case of 'Jatri Sauni' here. Due to the lack of coordination among the two organizations, the major purpose for which the 'Jatri Souni' was built was useless. As a result, ultimately the general public is deprived from availing the advantages of good urban services. So our hypothesis *'the more the contrast between democratic versus bureaucratic accountability, the more will be the problems of coordination in policy implementation,'* may said to be supported by the findings.

CONCLUSION

In this chapter an attempt was made to analyze how (a) how the central-local relationship and (b) how democratic vs. bureaucratic accountability influences inter-organizational coordination during policy implementation of urban governance of Bangladesh. We found that central-local relation affects the inter-organizational relationship. To some extent, it varies depending on the political identity of the Mayor of the City Corporation. Currently, in RCC the central-local relations do not create problems of coordination to a large extent as the Mayor belongs to the ruling party and he has good access to the central leadership. However, this good relationship is not enough to attract adequate financial grant from the central government. On the other hand, the contrast between democratic and bureaucratic governance creates inter-organizational coordination problems as both the organizations hold different modes of operation and accountability pattern which in the long run affects policy implementation of RCC.

NOTES

1. Analysis of this chapter is mainly based on information collected during interview with seven officials from government departments those are related to implementation of infrastructure policy of RCC. These officials include, Chairman, Executive Engineer and Town Planner from Rajshahi Development Authority (RDA), Executive Engineer and Deputy Divisional Engineer from Roads and Highways Department (R&HD), Executive Engineer and Assistant Executive Engineer from Local Government Engineering Department (LGED). However, in some cases, views from City Corporation officials have also been used for analysis.
2. Detailed discussion about the central-local relationship in urban governance in Bangladesh is made in the theoretical chapter. For more details see, Kamal Siddiqui (Ed.), Local Government in Bangladcsh (Revised second edition), Chapter VII, University press limited, Dhaka, Bangladesh, pp. 212-222.

3. Here, I have specially mentioned LGRD ministry because, like all the City Corporations, Rajshahi City Corporation works under this ministry. If the City Corporation authority wishes to communicate to the central-government, they must proceed through the LGRD ministry. That is why, central-local relationship in this research has been manifested by the strength of relationship that City Corporation has with the LGRD ministry.
4. Mayor is the executive and administrative head of the Rajshahi City Corporation who is elected directly by the people for every five years term.
5. BNP stands for Bangladesh Nationalist Party which is the second largest political party in ratio of vote getting in Bangladesh.
6. Nature in the sense that which party dominates the central power and political identity of the Mayor.
7. Legally, the City Corporation authority can not participate in the law making process. But, it is at least possible to incorporate inputs from City Corporation if the law makers desire. In Bangladesh, the tendency is that during law making or amendments, suggestions or inputs from the City Corporation are not inquired and if it is inquired, they are either ignored or by passed.
8. This case was discussed while interviewing the high ranking official of R&HD, Rajshahi.
9. 'Jatri Sauni' is a Bengali word which means waiting places for the passerby by the road side.
10. Laxmipur is the name of a place of Rajshahi City where the Medical College is situated.
11. BDT stands for Bangladeshi Taka (Name of the currency).
12. In the above arguments, it is noticeable that the bureaucrats tried to establish themselves as honest, responsible and neutral than that of the RCC authorities. But in actual practice, the scenario is different. The bureaucrats are equally dishonest and irresponsible like the RCC authorities.

7

CONCLUSIONS

This study was concerned about problems of coordination in policy implementation with regard to urban governance in Bangladesh. The main purpose of the study was to explore the causes of lack of coordination and how it affects policy implementation of urban government bodies. Coordination here is referred to sound working relationship and lack of coordination denotes problematic working environment within urban governance bodies and among various government organizations. Lack of coordination is discussed here from intra-organizational and inter-organizational perspective. Intra-organizational coordination means coordination within Rajshahi City Corporation and inter-organizational coordination is referred to coordination among RCC and different government organization that are involved with the policy implementation of RCC. Emphasis was given to explore how these relationships affect policy implementation of RCC.

The basic question that was asked, "how lack of intra and inter -organizational coordination affect policy implementation of urban governance in Bangladesh". The study tried to explore why problems of coordination occur in the policy implementation of urban governance? What impacts intra-organizational coordination and inter-organizational coordination have on policy implementation? With a view to answering these questions, a qualitative approach was adapted. Data were collected from officials of RCC as well as government offices. Structured open ended questionnaires were served to the respondents. Besides, few ward commissioners of RCC, few contractors who are involved with implementation of infrastructure policy of RCC, and few from the public were interviewed on the basis of random selection criteria. As part of qualitative enquiry, various secondary documents (books, journal and news papers), government documents and reports, documents of RCC were reviewed.

GENERAL FINDINGS OF THE STUDY

The policy subsystem of RCC is a complex issue. There are three most important actors in the policy subsystem of RCC. These are state, society and the Corporation Parishad. The state exerts some sort of indirect influence on the policy making through central government, political parties and the minister in charge of the Rajshahi. The Mayor is the chairman of the Corporation Parishad and belongs to the political party that runs the government at the center. That is why, the state to some extent can influence the policy making indirectly. On the other hand, the society does not have any influence on the policy making of RCC as civil society organizations in Rajshahi are very weak. As a result, policy process is mostly dominated by the Corporation Parishad. But, from the opinion of the respondents, it is found that policy making process of RCC is mostly dominated by the Mayor as he is supported by the majority of word commissioners. Regarding the implementation of infrastructure policy of RCC, it was observed that the Engineering Department can not perform alone. They are dependent on the Accounts Department and on the Press and Publication Department within RCC. However, the RCC deals with at least three government departments that are involved with implementation of infrastructure policy. These three departments are R&HD, LGED and RDA.

While talking about the lack of intra-organization coordination, two variables are important. These are lack of institutionalized rules and regulations and financial management. If the rules and regulations are not institutionalized, well defined and clearly spelled out about who would do what, then coordination becomes problematic. In this regard it is found that the RCC is administered by Rajshahi City Corporation Act, 1987 which is unclear in many respects and contains almost nothing regarding how to coordinate activities of different departments. Taking the advantages of this ambiguity, the laws are interpreted in different manner. This type of misinterpretation often creates problems of coordination.

This study also provides us some insight that financial management is also important for the intra-organizational coordination. We have found that RCC is suffering from inadequate financial resources. But, the demands for resources are many. The authorities, however, do not make proper distribution of available resources. Major portions of allocation go to those departments, whose heads maintain a close relationship with the Mayor and some influential ward commissioners which also create frustration among other departmental heads. This discontent also creates coordination problems within City Corporation.

With regard to the inter-organizational coordination, this study showed that central-local relations and democratic versus bureaucratic accountability are very important. It is found that the strength of central-local relationship is based on the political identity of the mayor. If the Mayor belongs to the government party, he receives more favours especially in terms of allocation of resources (how inadequate it may be) from the central government. But, if the Mayor belongs to the opposition, the scenario is just the opposite. Currently, the Mayor of the RCC holds more power as he has good access to the central leadership. That is why, there is positive relationship between RCC and central government which facilitate completion of many development projects. But, the situation was different during 1996-2001 when the Mayor was in the opposition. This study also depicts the biasness of the Rajshai City Corporation Act, 1987. The act keeps the provision of local autonomy for RCC leaving some sort of administrative and financial control in the hands of central government. The most controversial among the control mechanism is the power to issue circular, removal of the Mayor and the deputation of the CEO in the RCC etc. The central government always wants to keep the urban government bodies under pressure by using those mechanisms which are contradictory to ensuring local autonomy.

The contrast between democratic and bureaucratic accountability is also an important factor that determines the inter-organizational coordination. The study reveals that it is very difficult to ensure sound coordination among these two types of organization as their mode of operation and accountability pattern are different. The RCC is a political organ and administered by popularly elected Mayor. In constrast, government departments are staffed by the civil servants who are accountable to their line ministries in a hierarchic manner. In RCC, the decision making process is prompt as every action requires to be approved by the Mayor. But, in the case of government offices, matters relating to policy issue need to be approved by their line ministries. That is why, the decision making in government offices is lengthy. Problems of coordination start when the government offices do not respond quickly as expected by the RCC.

The study also found that the Mayor always tries to influence the government departments in order to get things done in his favour. The situation becomes more serious when the Mayor belongs to the ruling party. Not only the Mayor, even officials of the City Corporation try to influence government officials as we have seen in the case of 'Jatri Sauni' that has been discussed in the chapter six.

HOW THINGS GET IMPLEMENTED IN SITUATIONS OF LOW COORDINATION?

The whole process of policy implementation of RCC is strategic like a game. It's a situation where there is threat, persuasion, lobbying, reward and sanction mechanism. The process of policy implementation is not well coordinated. Decisions that are formulated and implemented may not reflect policy objectives that were emersioned at the outset.

A question may be asked, if there is no coordination, how work gets done and services provided. There must be some mechanisms behind it. The question is what is that mechanism? The answer is "one man show" that means the Mayor is all in all. He is the root of all powers and every thing gets done in his name. The second factor is a "solo dance" rather than a "well orchestrated" dance, which means that these departments act on their own and if some coordination happens its ok otherwise they go ahead. In this case policy outcome does not reflect policy objectives. Policy outcome leads to cost increase, delay in implementation and unsatisfactory service delivery etc.

Bibliography

BOOKS AND JOURNAL ARTICLES

Ahmed, N. (2002), *Privatization of State Owned Enterprises (SOS) in Bangladesh: A Study on Policy Implementation*, An Unpublished M.Phil Thesis, Department of Administration and Organization Theory, University of Bergen, Norway.

Ahmed, N. (2002), "Politicians and Bureaucrats in Local Government in Bangladesh: A Study of the Upazila Parishad" in Mahfuzul H. Chowdhury (Ed.), *Thirty Year of Bangladesh Politics: Essays in Memory of Dr. Mahfuzul Huq*, the University Press Limited, Dhaka, Bangladesh.

Ahmed, S.U. (1991), "Municipal Politics and Urban Developments in Dhaka, 1885-1915" in S.U. Ahmed (ed.), *Dhaka: Past Present Future*, Dhaka: Asiatic Society of Bangladesh, pp. 151-182.

Barret, S. and Fudge, C. (1981), "Examining the Policy-Action Relationship", in Barret, Susan and Fudge edited, *Policy and Action, Essays on the Implementation of Public Policy*, Methuen and Co. Ltd, London.

Brinkerhoff, W. D. and Arthur A. G. (2002), " Cientelism, Partrimonialism and democratic Governance: An Overview and Framework for Assessment and Programming", paper prepared for U.S Agency for International Development, Office for Democracy and Governance under Strategic Policy and Institutional Governance, Cambridge, USA.

Chowdhury, A.I. (1994), "Urban Administration and Finance in Bangladesh: A Review of Research", in N. Islam (ed.) *Urban Research in Bangladesh*, Dhaka: Center for Urban Studies, pp. 67-82.

Chowdhury, A. I. (1997), "Resource Mobilization and Urban Governance in Bangladesh", in Nazrul Islam et, al, (eds.) *Urban Governance in Bangladesh and Pakistan*, Center for Urban Studies, Dhaka, Bangladesh.

Constitution of the People's Republic of Bangladesh, Government of Bangladesh, Dhaka, 1991, p- 43.

Creswell, J. W. (1994), *Research Design: Qualitative and Quantitative Approaches*, Sage Publications, London.

Denzin, N. K. (1978), *The Research Act: A Theoretical Introduction to Sociological Methods* (2nd, ed.), New York, Magraw-Hill.

Elander, I. and Montin, S. (1990), "Decentralization and Control: Central-Local Government Relations in Sweden", *Policy and Politics*, 18, pp. 165-180.

Fayol, H. (1916), *General and Industrial Management*, Original Published in French; Translated 1949, Pitman Publishing, London.

Guetzkow, H. (1966), "Relations Among Organizations", in Raymond V. Bowers (ed.), *Studies on Behaviour in Organizations: A Research Symposium*, University of Georgia Press, Athens, GA.

Haque, M. M. (2003), *The Culture of Tadbir: The Building Bloch of Administrative Decisions in the Bangladesh Civil Service (BCS)*, An Unpublished M.Phil Thesis, Department of Administration and Organization Theory, University of Bergen, Norway.

Howlett, M. and Ramesh, M. (1995), *Studying Public Policy: Policy Cycles and Policy Subsystems*, Oxford University Press, Canada.

Huda, A.T.M.S. (1987), "Coordination in Public Administration: A Theoretical Analysis", in A.T.M. Shamsul Huda (ed.), *Coordination in Public Administration in Bangladesh*, Bangladesh Public Administration Training Center, Dhaka, Bangladesh.

Huq, M. *et al.* (2001), Policy Brief on *"Administrative Reform and Local Government"*, CPD Task Force Report, Centre for Policy Dialogue, Dhaka.

Hye, H. A. (ed.) (2000), *Governance: South Asian Perspective*, The University Press Limited, Dhaka.

Islam, N. (ed.) (1994), *Urban Research in Bangladesh: Review of Recent Trends and an Agenda for the 1990s*, Centre for Urban Studies, Dhaka.

Islam, N. (ed.) (2000), *Urban Governance in South Asia: Sub-regional and City Perspectives,* Centre for Urban Studies, Dhaka.

Islam, N. and Khan, M. M. (eds.) (1997), *Urban Governance in Bangladesh and Pakistan*, Centre for Urban Studies, Dhaka.

Jenkins, G. P., Roy, K. and Rup, K. (2000), "*Central-Local Fiscal Relations in Low Income Countries: The Case of Nepal*", CAER II Discussion Paper No. 69, Harvard Institute for International Development, Cambridge, USA (Retrieved from *http://www.cid.harvard.edu/caer2/htm/content/papers/paper69/paper69.htm).*

Jenkins, W. I. (1978), *Policy Analysis: A Political and Organizational Perspective*, Martin Robertson, London.

Jick, T. D. (1979), "Mixing Qualitative and Quantitative Methods: Triangulation in Action", *Administrative Science Quarterly*, No. 24, pp. 602-611.

John, P. (2002), *Recent Trends in Central-Local Government Relations*, Policy Studies Institute (PSI), London, U.K. (Retrieved from *www.psi.org.uk/publications/publication.asp?publication_id=166).*

Karim, A. (2000), *Recent Changes in the Structure of the Union Parishad in Bangladesh: Scope for Participation of Women*, An Unpublished M.Phil Thesis, Department of Administration and Organization Theory, University of Bergen, Norway.

Kaufmann, F. (ed.) (1991), *The Challenge: Problems as Contestable Issues*, Walter de Gruyter, Berlin, New York.

Khan, M. M. (1994a), "Urban Development in Developing Countries with Special Reference to Bangladesh", *Asian Affairs*, 16(2), pp, 5-17.

Khan, M. M. (1996), Urban Local Governance in Bangladesh: An Overview, *Journal of Administration and Diplomacy*, Vol. 4, No. 1, January-June.

Khan, M. M. (1997), "Urban Local Governance in Bangladesh: An Overview", in Nazrul Islam and M.M. Khan (eds) *Urban Governance in Bangladesh and Pakistan*, Centre for Urban Studies, Dhaka.

Khan, M. M. *et, al,* (1997a), *Central-Local Relations in Urban Governance: A Study of Two City Corporations in Bangladesh*, The Bergen-Dhaka

Administrative Project, Stream # 2, Department of Public Administration, University of Dhaka.

Khan, M. M. (2002), "Political and Administrative Corruption: Concepts, Comparative Experiences and Bangladesh Case", A paper prepared for Transparency International - Bangladesh Chapter, Department of Public Administration, University of Dhaka, Bangladesh.

Khan, S. (1995), *Elusiveness of Coordination at Sub-national Level: A Focus on BRDB*, Academy Publishers, Dhaka, Bangladesh.

Kjellberg, F. (1995), "The Changing Values of Local Government" in Teune, H. (ed.) *Local Governance Around the World*, The Annals of the American Academy of Political and Social science, Thousand Oaks, Sage.

Levine, S. and Paul E. W. (1962), "Exchange as a Conceptual Framework for the Study of Inter-Organizational Relations", *Administrative Science Quarterly*, Vol. 6, No. 4, pp. 683-651.

Local Government in Asia and the Pacific: A Comparative Study, Country Report, Bangladesh, United National Economic and Social Commission for Asia and the Pacific, *(http://www.unescap.org/huset/lgstudy/country/bangladesh/bangladesh.html#top)*.

March, J. G. and Herbert A. S. (1958), *Organizations*, Wiley, New York.

March, J. G. and Olsen, J. P. (1989), *Rediscovering Institutions: The Organizational Basis of Politics*, Free Press, New York.

Marrett, Cora, (1971), "On the Specification of Inter-organizational Dimensions", *Sociology and Social Research*, Vol. 6, No. 4, pp. 83-99.

McCarney, P. L. H. and Rodriguez, A. (1995), Towards an Understanding of Governance: The Emergence of an Idea and its Implications for urban Research in Developing Countries", in R. Stren and J.K. Dell (eds), *Urban Research in the Developing World*, Vol. 4 Perspectives on the City, Toronto: The Centre for Ur ban and Community Studies, University of Toronto.

McLaughlin, Milbrey W. (1985), "Implementation Realities and Evaluation Design" in R.L. Shotland and M.M. Mark (eds.), *Social Science and Social Policy*, Beverly Hills: Sage.

McMaster, J. (1993): *Urban Financial Management*, EDI Technical Materials, Washington D.C, The World Bank.

Merriam, S. B. (1988), *Case Study Research in Education: A Qualitative Approach,* San Francisco: Jossey-Bass.

Meter, D. S. V. and Horn, C. L. V. (1975), "The Policy Implementation Process: A Conceptual Framework", *The Journal of Administration and Society*, Vol. 6, No. 4, February 1975, Sage Publication.

Miller, E. J. (1959), Technology, Territory and Time: The Internal Differentiation of Complex Production Systems, *Human Relations.*

Mintzberg, H. (1979), *The Structuring of Organization*, Prentice-Hall, Englewood Cliffs.

Mohit, M. A. (1992), "Institutional Management for the Development of Dhaka Metropolitan Area: Problems and Prospects" in N. Islam and A.I. Chowdhury (eds.), *Urban Land Management in Bangladesh*, Dhaka, Ministry of Land, Government of Bangladesh.

Montin, S. and Erik, A. (eds.) (2000), *Towards a New Concept of Local Self-Government? Recent Local Government Legislation in Comparative Perspective*, Fagbokforlaget, Bergen, Norway.

Mott, D. F. B. (1968), "Coordination and Inter-Organization Relations in Health", in Paul E. White and George Vlasok (eds.) *Inter-Organizational Research in Health,* Baltimore; JOHNS Hopkins University School of Hygiene and Public Health.

Murtaza, M. G. (2002), *Urban Governance in Bangladesh*, Published by A.K.Sultana Murtaza, Khulna, Bangladesh.

Page, E. C. (1991), *Localism and Centralism in Europe. The Political and Legal Bases of Local-self Government*, Oxford, Oxford University Press.

Prud'home, R. (1995), Megacities Management: Institutional Dimensions, in J. Stubbs and G Clarke (eds.), *Megacity Management in the Asian and Pacific Region*, Vol. 1, Asian Development Bank, Manila.

Punch, K. (1998), *Introduction to Social Research: Quantitative and Qualitative Approaches*, Sage Publication.

Rahman, M. S. (1989), "Challenges to the City Government in Bangladesh: A Case of Rajshahi City Corporation", *The Journal of Local Government*, National Institute of Local Government, Vol. 18, No. 1. January-June, Dhaka, Bangladesh.

Rhodes, R. A. W. (1997), *Understanding Governance: Policy Networks, Governance, Reflexibility and Accountability*, Buckingham: Open University Press.

Robinson, D. *et. al*, (eds.) (2000), *Managing Development: Understanding Inter-Organizational Relationships*, Sage Publications in Association with the Open University, London.

Schlager, E. (1999), "A Comparison of Frameworks, Theories, and Models of Policy Process" in Paul A. Sabatier (edt) *Theories of the Policy Process*, Oxford: Westview Press.

Selznick, P. (1957), *Leadership in Administration: A Sociological Interpretation*, Harper and Row, New York.

Sharpe, L. J. (1970), "Theories and Values of Local Government", *Political Studies*, Vol. XVIII, No. 2, pp. 153-174.

Siddique, K. (ed.), (1994), *Local Government in South Asia: A Comparative Perspective*, Dhaka: University Press Limited.

Siddique, K. (ed.), (1994), *Local Government in Bangladesh*, Dhaka: University Press Limited.

Siddique, Kamal, *et. al*, (eds.) (2000), *Overcoming The Governance Crisis in Dhaka City*, The University Press Limited, Dhaka.

Task Force on Urban Governance, National Policy Forum (2001), CUS Bulletin on Urbanization and Development, Centre for Urban Studies, Vol. 41, July-December, Dhaka.

The Rajshahi City Corporation Act, 1987, Government of Bangladesh, Ministry of Local Government, Rural Development and Cooperatives, Dhaka.

Thompson, J. D. (1967), *Organizations in Action*, New York; McGraw Hill Book Co.

UNDP/HABITAT, (1992), *Dhaka Metropolitan Development Planning (DMDP): Report on Institutional Issue*, Dhaka: Mott, MacDonald Ltd, and Others, November.

Urban Edge, (1984), Urban Edge: Issues and Innovations, Washington D.C., The World Bank.

USAID, (1999), *A Handbook on Fighting Corruption*, Washington, DC: U.S. Agency for International Development, Center for Democracy and Governance, Technical Publication Series, February.

Weber, M. (1947), *The Theory of Social and Economic Organization*, trans. A. M. Henderson and Talcott Parsons. New York: Free Press.

Wilson, W. (1987), "The Study of Administration", *Political Science Quarterly*, Vol. 2, pp. 197-222.

World Bank, (1985), *Bangladesh: An Agenda for Tax Reform* (in Three Volumes), Executive Summary and Overview, Washington D.C, The World Bank.

Yin, R. K., (1994), *Case Study Research: Design and Methods*, (2nd Edition), Thousand Oaks, CA, Sage Publication.

Zafarullah, Habib *et, al*, (1997), "Civil Service System: Bangladesh", Paper presented in Civil Service Systems in Comparative Perspective, Indiana University, Bloomington, Indiana, April 5-8, (Retrieved from *http://www.indiana.edu/~csrc/zafar1.html*).

NEWSPAPERS

The Holiday, (An English weekly) Internet Edition, Country News, 26 September, 2003 *(www.weeklyholiday.net/260903/count.html)*.

Sonali Sangbad (A Rajshahi based local dailies), 20 October, 2002, 20 December, 2002.

The Daily Star (An English daily), Internet Edition, 16 November, 1999, 12 March, 2003, Dhaka *(www.thedailystar.net)*.

The Independent (An English Daily), Internet Edition, 09 May, 2003, Dhaka *(www.independent-bangladesh.com)*.

WEB PAGES

www.cid.harvard.edu/caer2/htm/content/papers/paper69/paper69.htm

www.psi.org.uk/publications/publication.asp?publication_id=166

www.unescap.org/huset/lgstudy/country/bangladesh/bangladesh.html#top

www.indiana.edu/~csrc/zafar1.html

www.utmb.edu/dci/JARGON/RV.htm#Validity

www.geocities.com/~profwork/pp/implement/define.html

ABBREVIATIONS

AL	Awami League
BNP	Bangladesh Nationalist Party
BRTA	Bangladesh Road and Transport Authority
CDA	Chittagong Development Authority
CEE	Chief Executive Engineer
CEO	Chief Executive Officer
CUS	Center for Urban Studies
CWASA	Chittagong Water and Sewerage Authority
DCC	Dhaka City Corporation
DESA	Dhaka Electricity Supply Authority
DMA	Dhaka Metropolitan Area
DMP	Dhaka Metropolitan Police
DPHE	Department of Public Health Engineering
DWASA	Dhaka Water and Sewerage Authority
GS	Gram Sarkar (Village Government)
KDA	Khulna Development Authority
LGED	Local Government Engineering Department
LGRD&C	Local Government, Rural Development and Cooperatives

MPWH	Ministry of Public Works and Housing
PDB	Power Development Board
PWD	Public Works Department
PWDB	Power and Water Development Board
RCC	Rajshahi City Corporation
RDA	Rajshahi Development Authority
R&HD	Roads and Highways Department
RAJUK	Rajdhani Unnayan Kartripakkha (Capital Development Authority)
UDD	Urban Development Directorate
UNO	Upazila Nirbahi Officer